Collecting
Presidential Dollars

Whitman Publishing, LLC
Atlanta, GA

© 2007 Whitman Publishing, LLC
3101 Clairmont Road · Suite C · Atlanta, GA 30329

OCG™ collecting guide

Correspondence concerning this book may be directed to the publisher, Attn: Whitman Insider Guides, at the address above.

ISBN: 0794823920
Printed in China

Disclaimer: Expert opinion should be sought in any significant numismatic purchase. This book is presented as a guide only. No warranty or representation of any kind is made concerning the completeness of the information presented.

WCG™ valuations grid

For a complete catalog of numismatic reference books, supplies, and storage products, visit Whitman Publishing online at:

www.whitman**books**.com

Table of Contents

Launched in 2007 with the George Washington dollar, the series of presidential dollar coins has already become a "must have" collectible for numismatists and the general public. By 2016, all presidents who have been deceased for at least two years will be showcased (at the rate of four new designs each year). The progress will follow history: Washington, Adams, Jefferson, and Madison, continuing into the modern era. Likely, the talented United States Mint staff will create most if not all of the images. The first was by John Mercanti. The reverse of each presidential dollar will show the Statue of Liberty, officially designated as *Liberty Enlightening the World,* one of America's best-known icons, as interpreted by Mint sculptor-engraver Don Everhart.

The coins are of a distinctive hue—"golden dollars," as they have been called, although the alloy contains no gold metal. The distinctive composition follows that introduced by the Sacagawea dollar in 2000: a copper core with bonded outer layers of manganese brass (77% copper, 12% zinc, 7% manganese, 4% nickel). The result is a bright, lustrous coin.

The presidential dollars are further unusual in that the *edge* of each is lettered with the two national mottoes: IN GOD WE TRUST and E PLURIBUS UNUM. In addition, on the edge the date is given as well as a mintmark identifying where it was struck, such as P for Philadelphia and D for Denver. Dating the coins on the edge is indeed unusual. Collectors can keep them in order by the inscription on the obverse, "1st President" for Washington, for example.

HISTORICAL MONEY DEPICTING PRESIDENTS

The use of presidential portraits on coins, tokens, medals, and paper money has a long and rich tradition dating back to George Washington, whose image appeared on more than a dozen different privately issued coins during his lifetime, and many more since then, including the present-day quarter dollar (launched in 1932 and still going strong, including the statehood reverse designs of 1999 to date). Washington has also been a paper-money favorite, including on the dollar bill. When the Philadelphia Mint struck its first coins for circulation in 1793, a portrait of Washington was suggested, following the tradition used by the reigning kings and queens of Europe. He rejected the idea as "too monarchial," and a depiction of Miss Liberty was used instead.

Now with the "golden dollar" joining in, all of our currently circulating coins show such leaders, including the Lincoln cent (1909 to date), Jefferson nickel (1938 to date), Roosevelt dime (1945 to date), Washington quarter, and Kennedy half dollar (1964 to date). Going back a few years, Dwight D. Eisenhower appeared on circulating dollar coins from 1971 to 1978.

1926 Sesquicentennial half dollar

While today it is not legal to use the portrait of a living person on paper money, there is no such restriction on coins. However, only one president was so illustrated during his lifetime: Calvin Coolidge, who appeared with Washington on the 1926 Sesquicentennial (150th anniversary) of American Independence commemorative half dollar.

While only a few presidents have appeared on pocket-change coins, quite a few have been honored on special commemoratives. Many numismatists collect such coins, which were first made in 1892 (the first president to be depicted was Washington on a 1900 commemorative silver dollar that also featured French general and Revolutionary War hero Lafayette). Many official medals, struck at the U.S. Mint, have featured the chief executive. These include Indian peace medals presented to Native Americans through much of the 19th century, inaugural medals, and many different honors and awards. More numerous are privately minted medals, of which hundreds of different were made for Washington alone.

Current paper money illustrates presidents Washington ($1), Jefferson ($2), Lincoln ($5), Jackson ($20), and Grant ($50). Two denominations show other national figures: Alexander Hamilton on the $10 and Benjamin Franklin on the $100.

THE PRESIDENCY: A RICH HISTORY

The American government is divided into three decision-making branches: the executive, legislative, and judicial. The president or chief executive is an individual, while the legislative branch with the Senate and House of Representatives includes more than 500 elected officials, and the judicial branch, the Supreme Court, has nine. Each is part of a checks-and-balances system to regulate and temper the actions of the others.

The office of president was established when the Constitution was ratified in 1788. This document, which has been amended over the years, sets forth the duties of each branch and how members are chosen. Our first president, Washington, was chosen by Congress and subsequently served two terms, 1789 to 1793 and 1793 to 1797. The first popular election for president took place in 1796, with John Adams the winner. The fathers of the Constitution, perhaps fearful that the general public might make an unwise decision, set up the Electoral College, consisting of electors chosen by each state. These electors typically follow the popular vote within their state, casting a unanimous ballot for the favorite. In several instances, presidential candidates who did not win the popular vote were chosen by the Electoral College.

In early elections the runner up in votes, from the opposing political party, became the vice president. The impracticality of this was realized, and a constitutional amendment in 1804 provided that both the president and vice president are to be chosen from the same ticket. Political parties, which have changed over the years, are now dominated by the Democrats and Republicans. Gone are the Federalists, Whigs, and others once prominent.

Each party has a nominating convention in the summer of an election year, with the November contest in the offing. Favorites are presented for consideration, and delegates to the convention cast votes. In some instances, the nominations are made quickly. In others, many ballots are taken until, finally, a candidate is chosen. Most notably, at the Democratic convention in 1850 there was no clear choice, and only on the 48th ballot was Franklin Pierce chosen—a so-called "dark horse" candidate. It has been tradition that if a sitting president stands for a second term, his party will nominate him to run. This does not assure a victory in the November election. President Gerald Ford lost when he ran for a second term in 1976 and Jimmy Carter lost his reelection bid in 1980.

After securing the nomination of his party the presidential candidate selects his running mate. The election is held in early November. The popular votes are tallied, after which the Electoral College chooses the winner, the inauguration is held, historically the following March, but moved up in the early 20th century to January, to minimize the "lame duck" period after the election, a time when the sitting president is making the transition to leave office.

Elections are held every four years. Until a 1951 constitutional amendment set the limit as two terms, there were no such restrictions. The only president to be elected more than twice was Franklin D. Roosevelt, the winner in the contests of 1932, 1936, 1940, and 1944, with a different vice presidential running mate each time, per his choice.

If a president dies in office, his vice president is the automatic successor. This has happened several times in history, beginning with William Henry Harrison, who was inaugurated in March 1841, but died a month later, and was succeeded by his vice president, James Tyler.

**Abraham Lincoln,
one of four assassinated presidents**

Four presidents have been assassinated: Abraham Lincoln (1865), James Garfield (1881), William McKinley (1901), and John F. Kennedy (1963). One president has resigned: Richard M. Nixon in 1974. He had no vice president, as the man holding that office, Spiro T. Agnew, had earlier resigned in a scandal. Succeeding Nixon was Gerald R. Ford, minority leader of the House of Representatives—the only president who was never elected to the office of either president or vice president.

When Washington was inaugurated in 1789, New York City was the seat of the federal government. Philadelphia was the next capital. Washington, DC, first known as the Federal City, became the capital in 1800. James Madison and his wife Dolley were the first president and first lady to live in the White House, which at the time had not been completed. The first White House was burned by the British in 1814, near the end of the War of 1812, after which the present White House was constructed.

Each president is given a salary, which was $25,000 annually until 1873, when it was raised to $50,000, then to $75,000 in 1909, $100,000 in 1949, $200,000 in 1969, and $400,000 in 2001. In addition, the expenses of operating the White House are paid for, as are costs associated with presidential duties, including travel and entertainment. Each president names his Cabinet, a committee of advisors. The Cabinet positions have varied in number, name, and responsibility over the years.

White House state dinner, 1870

The president's wife, known as the first lady, usually takes responsibility for planning entertainment at the White House. There has been one bachelor president, James Buchanan (1857–1861). Grover Cleveland was the only president to have his wedding ceremony in the White House, in 1886. Cleveland was also the only president to serve two non-consecutive terms. He was the 22nd president and also the 24th. Several presidents have been widowers, in which instances a lady relative has helped with first lady functions. The most famous first lady was probably Jacqueline ("Jackie") Kennedy; without doubt she graced more magazine covers than any other. There are no restrictions as to the gender of a president, and many hope that some day a woman will be in that position, in which instance we may have a "first gentleman" in the White House as well.

Many presidents were trained in law or rose through military ranks. Being a military hero propelled Washington, Jackson, and Eisenhower, among others, into the White House. Woodrow Wilson was an educator, Warren Harding a businessman, Jimmy Carter a peanut farmer, and Ronald Reagan a movie actor. Two modern presidents have preferred to use nicknames while conducting official duties: Jimmy Carter and Bill Clinton.

Two pairs of presidents have been father and son: John Adams and John Quincy Adams, and George H.W. Bush and George W. Bush. There were two Roosevelt presidents, Theodore and Franklin, distantly related. Ditto for William Henry Harrison and Benjamin Harrison.

Several presidents are remembered by well-known monuments, including the Jefferson Memorial and the Lincoln Memorial, both in Washington, DC. For modern presidents, libraries have been established, usually near where they lived in private life. These contain documents, records, and memorabilia and are open to the public. The Mount Rushmore National Monument in South Dakota has the sculptured images of Washington, Jefferson, Theodore Roosevelt, and Lincoln. A state is named after George Washington, and many towns and counties bear the names of various other early chief executives. The state now known as Colorado was once Jefferson Territory.

The historical evaluation of presidents admits of a large amount of opinion. Washington is generally admired by all, Lincoln is a favorite with many (but not necessarily in the South), Harding is viewed as incompetent, Nixon as scarred by scandal, and so it goes. The presidency of Theodore Roosevelt is certainly one of the more interesting to contemplate, while there is little to be remembered about, say, Franklin Pierce. Among early presidents, there is probably more division of opinion on Jackson than any other. Franklin D. Roosevelt probably takes the honors for having the most dynamic presidency in an era which included the Depression  and World War II; he was also in office the longest, from 1933 to 1945. Harry S Truman (who had no middle name, but just an initial without a period) was widely considered to be a "lesser" president, until serious reevaluation of him in our own generation. Today, his legacy is admired. No doubt you have your own particular favorites.

As the presidential "golden dollars" are produced and each past executive comes in for a new measure of fame, it is interesting to contemplate the lives of those depicted. The following biographies have basic information about each president together with a selection of lesser-known facts and sidelights.

George Washington

February 22, 1732 – December 14, 1799

Political party: None

Vice president: John Adams, 1789 to 1797

First lady: Married widow Martha Dandridge Custis in 1759. The couple had two children by Martha's first marriage: John "Jack" Parke Custis and Martha "Patsy" Custis.

Especially remembered for: Leadership during the Revolutionary War. Defining the duties of the office of president. "The Father of Our Country." His sterling character, which served as a shining example of integrity. Most popular president in terms of the number of different coins, tokens, medals, and currency notes with his portrait. One of four presidents honored on Mount Rushmore.

George Washington, our first and most famous president, was born in Virginia to a well-to-do family. He learned surveying, then served with British forces in the French and Indian War. In the American Revolutionary War he served as commander-in-chief of the United States Army. His forcing of the British to evacuate Boston, the privations of winter camp in Valley Forge, the crossing of the icy Delaware River, and other difficulties and triumphs became part of history. In 1781, with the aid of French allies and the assistance of the Marquis de Lafayette, he forced the surrender of British general Cornwallis at Yorktown.

Washington was chairman of the Constitutional Convention in 1787 and 1788. After ratification of the Constitution, the Electoral College named him as our first president. It was his task and challenge to develop the first Cabinet, to work with Congress and the Supreme Court, and to establish procedures for the presidency. At the time the seat of the federal government was in New York City.

When the French Revolution was followed by war between England and France, Washington ignored the recommendations of Secretary of State Thomas Jefferson and Secretary of the Treasury Alexander Hamilton and insisted upon a neutral stance. In his farewell address he recommended that in the future the country avoid "entangling alliances."

By the 1796 election, two political parties had developed, setting the scene for a contest. In 1797 Washington retired to his Mount Vernon estate on the banks of the Potomac River, where he lived until dying of a throat infection on December 14, 1799. In 1800, funeral medals inscribed HE IS IN GLORY, THE WORLD IN TEARS were issued in his memory.

Portrait of George Washington as general, engraved by Asher B. Durand after a painting by Trumbull. (*National Portrait Gallery of Distinguished Americans,* Vol. I, 1834)

Washington funeral medal by Jacob Perkins, 1800. The reverse gives abbreviated dates of his life and career. Holed at the top, these were worn on ribbons in parades. (Actual size 29.2 mm)

John Adams

October 30, 1735 – July 4, 1826

Political party: Federalist

Vice president: Thomas Jefferson

First lady: Married Abigail Smith on October 25, 1764. The couple had five children: Abigail Amelia Adams; John Quincy Adams (who became president); Susanna Adams; Charles Adams; and Thomas Boylston Adams.

Especially remembered for: First president to compete in a national election. The XYZ Affair.

John Adams was born in Norfolk, Massachusetts, son of John and Susanna Boylston Adams. He studied law and graduated from Harvard in 1755. Inspired with patriotic fervor, he served in the Continental Congress from 1774 to 1778. He was commissioner to France in 1778, minister to the Netherlands in 1780, and chief negotiator in the 1783 peace treaty. Later, he was minister to England from 1785 to 1788, and vice president of the United States under George Washington, 1789 to 1797. In the 1796 election, his rival Thomas Jefferson came within three Electoral College votes of being named president. Due to a flaw in the Constitution (later corrected), the loser became his vice president, creating much friction.

When Adams became president, the war between the French and British was causing great difficulties for the United States on the high seas and sparking intense differences among political factions within America. Adams sent three commissioners to France to try to quiet matters, but in spring 1798 it was learned that French foreign minister Talleyrand and the Directory refused to negotiate unless the United States paid a bribe. Adams reported the dire matter to Congress. Correspondence was made public, in which the Frenchmen seeking bribes were named only as "X," "Y," and "Z." The XYZ Affair became the cause of the day, and Adams's stance against the extortion made him a popular hero. By the time of the 1800 election, his Federalist party was divided on matters of foreign policy, while the opposing Republicans were united in their stance.

During Adams's administration the seat of the government was moved from New York City to Washington City, District of Columbia, later simply called Washington. He was the first president to live in the White House, arriving on November 1, 1800, just before the next presidential election. In a letter to his wife, he stated, "I pray Heaven to bestow the best of Blessings on this House and all that shall hereafter inhabit it. May none but honest and wise Men ever rule under this roof." After his presidency, Adams retired to his farm in Quincy, Massachusetts. He died the same day as his old political rival Thomas Jefferson: the fourth of July, 1826.

The Adams family house in Braintree (now known as Quincy), Massachusetts.

Thomas Jefferson

April 13, 1743 – July 4, 1826

Political party: Democrat-Republican

Vice presidents: Aaron Burr, 1801 to 1805; George Clinton, 1805 to 1809

Wife: Married 22-year-old widow Martha Wayles Skelton on January 1, 1772. The couple had six children: Martha Washington Jefferson (called "Patsy"); Jane Randolph Jefferson; infant son (1777); Mary Jefferson (called "Polly"); Lucy Elizabeth Jefferson (died in infancy); and Lucy Elizabeth Jefferson (second daughter with that name). Mrs. Jefferson died in 1781. There was no spousal "first lady" in his White House, although his daughter, Patsy—by then Mrs. Thomas Mann Randolph— stayed there for protracted periods and helped with entertaining. She gave birth to a son there.

Especially remembered for: Drafting the Declaration of Independence. Work on finance during the Washington administration. His Embargo Act of 1807 was widely considered to be a failure. Jefferson designed his home (Monticello) and other buildings considered to be high examples of architecture. Nicknames: "Man of the People," "Sage of Monticello." One of four presidents honored on Mount Rushmore. Portrait widely used on U.S. coins (nickels) and paper money (especially the $2 denomination).

Thomas Jefferson was born in Shadwell, Virginia, to a prosperous family. His father, Peter Jefferson, owned a plantation of 5,000 acres, which eventually passed to his son. His mother, Jane Randolph Jefferson, was well known in society.

Thomas graduated from the College of William and Mary in 1762, and afterward studied law. Of a literary turn of mind, Jefferson read widely and built a memorable library (later to become a part of the Library of Congress).

Jefferson was talented as a writer, less so as an orator. Most of his contributions to the Virginia House of Burgesses and the Continental Congress were letters and documents, including many with astute recommendations of policy. In 1776 he drafted the Declaration of Independence. After the Revolutionary War he was governor of Virginia and, later, minister to France. In 1786 his draft of an act allowing religious freedom was signed into law. His sympathy for the French Revolution led him into conflict with Alexander Hamilton when Jefferson was the first secretary of state in Washington's Cabinet, a post he resigned in 1793. In 1796 Jefferson ran for president,

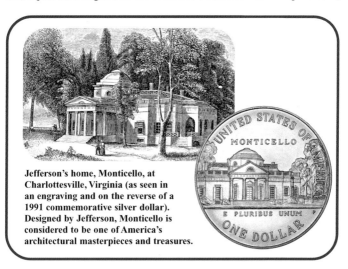

Jefferson's home, Monticello, at Charlottesville, Virginia (as seen in an engraving and on the reverse of a 1991 commemorative silver dollar). Designed by Jefferson, Monticello is considered to be one of America's architectural masterpieces and treasures.

but lost by three Electoral College votes to John Adams. Due to a flaw in the Constitution (later corrected), Jefferson as runner up became vice president.

In 1800 the House of Representatives settled an Electoral College tie, naming Jefferson as president and Aaron Burr as vice president. Burr later became involved in deep scandal and condemnation.

Jefferson opposed a strong centralized government and advocated the rights of states for most matters, bringing decisions closer to the people. By the time of his inauguration in 1801 (the first such ceremony to take place in Washington), earlier political conflict with France had ceased. When the Barbary pirates sought to exact tribute from American vessels on the Mediterranean, the president sent forces to "the halls of Tripoli." He engineered the purchase of the Louisiana Territory from France, despite questions of its constitutionality. He also reduced the federal debt by a third and made many internal improvements. Seeking to keep American vessels from depredations during the Napoleonic Wars between England and France, Jefferson signed the Embargo Act in 1807. This proved to be a disaster for American commerce and precipitated many difficulties.

After his presidency, Jefferson retired to Monticello, where he became an active correspondent with government leaders, participated in the design of buildings for the University of Virginia, and spent time in cultural and leisure activities. He died the same day as his old political rival John Adams: the fourth of July, 1826.

Portrait of Thomas Jefferson from a Bureau of Engraving and Printing vignette book, 1876.

James Madison

March 16, 1751 – June 28, 1836

Political party: Democrat-Republican

Vice presidents: George Clinton, 1809 to 1812; none 1812 and 1813; Elbridge Gerry, 1813 and 1814; none 1814 to 1817

First lady: Married Dolley Payne Todd on September 15, 1794. The couple had no children.

Especially remembered for: Making a major contribution to the ratification of the Constitution by writing, with Alexander Hamilton and John Jay, the Federalist essays. Nickname: "Father of the Constitution." Strong proponent of the Bill of Rights. His wife Dolley became one of the best-remembered first ladies.

James Madison was born in Port Conway, King George County, Virginia, son of James and Nelly Conway Madison. He spent his youth in the same state, entered Princeton (then the College of New Jersey), and took his degree in 1771. Madison studied history and law. When the Virginia Constitution was framed in 1776, he helped with its provisions.

Madison participated in the framing of the Virginia Constitution in 1776, and from 1780 to 1783 he was a member of the Continental Congress. This was followed by service in the Virginia Legislature. Madison was a delegate to the Constitutional Convention in 1787. As a representative to Congress he helped frame the Bill of Rights and the first federal revenue bill. He was outspoken concerning Alexander Hamilton's financial proposals, which he felt would concentrate wealth in the hands of Northern interests. From this opposition the

Republican party arose. Under Thomas Jefferson, Madison was secretary of state from 1801 to 1809—a particularly trying time in international relations, especially after the 1807 Embargo Act became law.

Madison was elected president in 1808. Before he took office the Embargo Act was repealed. During the first year of his administration, the United States prohibited trade with warring Britain and France; then in May, 1810, Congress authorized trade with both, directing the president, if either would accept America's view of neutral rights, to forbid trade with the other nation. Napoleon acceded, and in late 1810 Madison proclaimed non-intercourse with Great Britain. Relations worsened as British ships seized American cargoes and kidnapped ("impressed") American sailors. On June 1, 1812, at Madison's request, Congress declared war.

The War of 1812 saw military engagements at sea, on the Great Lakes, and in the British invasion of Maryland and Washington, where the White House, Capitol, and other buildings were burned.

Madison's home, Montpelier, as shown on the reverse of a 1993-S commemorative dollar.

The tide turned with the unsuccessful bombardment of Baltimore, and the enemy troops went home. Peace was declared in December 1814, but before the news reached America, the Battle of New Orleans was fought in January 1815, with General Andrew Jackson scoring a sound victory.

After his presidency, James Madison retired to his estate, Montpelier, in Virginia.

James Monroe

April 28, 1758 – July 4, 1831

Political party: Democrat-Republican

Vice president: Daniel D. Tompkins, 1817 to 1825

First lady: Married Elizabeth "Eliza" Kortright on February 16, 1786. The couple had three children: Eliza Kortright Monroe (1786–1835); James Spence Monroe (1799–1800); and Maria Hester Monroe (1803–1850).

Especially remembered for: The Era of Good Feelings. The Missouri Compromise bill. The Monroe Doctrine (the name assigned years later to this policy). In 1923 the latter was celebrated by a special commemorative half dollar.

James Monroe was born in Westmoreland County, Virginia, son of Spence and Elizabeth Jones Monroe. In 1776 he graduated from the College of William and Mary, after which he joined the Continental Army, distinguishing himself in the Revolution. He then practiced law in Virginia. A member of the Continental Congress from 1783 to 1786, he was also prominent in state politics and was among those who ratified the Constitution. In 1790 he was elected as a United States senator, serving until 1794, after which he was minister to France until 1796. Continuing in public service, he was governor of Virginia from 1799 to 1802, minister to France and England from 1803 to 1807 (participating in the 1803 Louisiana Purchase negotiations), secretary of state from 1811 to 1817, and for part of the time (1814 and 1815), concurrently the secretary of war.

With the endorsement of incumbent Madison, Monroe was named as the Republican candidate for president in 1816. He won the election handily, as he also did with his bid for reelection in 1820. After entering the White House, he started on a goodwill tour, winding through the Northeast. The nation was weary from the War of 1812 and from depressed economic conditions, and Monroe's administration was viewed as ushering in the "Era of Good Feelings." His tour had very little pomp and circumstance. At each stop he was greeted by state and local dignitaries and made to feel welcome, but without fanfare.

Unfortunately, economic conditions took a downturn in 1818 and 1819, causing much rancor in Congress and elsewhere, although Monroe himself remained popular. In 1819 Missouri Territory's application to join the Union as a slave-holding state failed, setting off two years of controversy. The result was the Missouri Compromise, which kept the North-South political balance by admitting Missouri as a slavery state and at the same time Maine as a free state. Under its provisions, slavery was prohibited to the west and north of Missouri.

On the international scene at the time, Spain was maneuvering to re-acquire its former territories in Latin America, and Russia had territorial ambitions. In 1821, Spain ceded Florida to the United States. To put an end to further imperialism in the Western Hemisphere the famous Monroe Doctrine of 1823 stated that ". . . the American continents, by the free and independent condition which they have assumed and maintain, are henceforth not to be considered as subjects for future colonization by any European power."

Monroe left the White House in 1825. He died in New York City in 1831 on the fourth of July.

John Quincy Adams

July 11, 1767 – February 23, 1848

Political party: Democrat-Republican

Vice president: John C. Calhoun, 1825 to 1829

First lady: Married Louisa Catherine Johnson on July 26, 1797. The couple had four children: George Washington Adams (1801–1829); John Adams (1803–1834); Charles Francis Adams (1807–1886); and Louisa Catherine Adams (1811–1812).

Especially remembered for: His foreign ministry, development of the country's infrastructure, and support of literature, art, and science.

John Quincy Adams was born in Braintree, Massachusetts, to John and Abigail Smith Adams, eventually becoming the first son of a president to be elected to the same office. As a youth he watched the 1775 Battle of Bunker Hill from a vantage point above the family farm. He grew into a man of literary talent, widely read and fluent in several languages. He accompanied his father to Europe, acting as his secretary and keeping a particularly detailed diary.

In 1787 Adams graduated from Harvard College, after which he practiced law. In 1794 he was named as minister to the Netherlands, after which he served as minister to Prussia through 1801. Elected to the United States Senate in 1802, he served until 1808. He was minister to Russia from 1809 to 1811, and was the peace commissioner at Ghent, Belgium, in 1814 at the settlement of the War of 1812. Under James Monroe he was secretary of state through 1825, serving with great distinction, including arranging the cession of Florida from Spain in 1821, negotiation with Great Britain for the joint control of the Oregon Territory, and helping formulate what became known as the Monroe Doctrine.

In 1824 he was one of several candidates for president, the field also including War of 1812 hero Andrew Jackson, William H. Crawford, and Henry Clay. None attained a majority of Electoral College votes, and the matter was put before Congress, which decided for Adams, largely through the influence of Henry Clay. Adams named Clay as secretary of state, provoking great antagonism from Jackson backers, who called it a "corrupt bargain." As president, Adams faced much opposition by Congress, but was able to institute important programs, including setting up a network of roads and canals. He strongly supported education, art, and science.

John Quincy Adams is seen on the 1923 Monroe Doctrine Centennial commemorative half dollar.

The presidential contest of 1828 pitted Adams against Jackson. The election was hard fought, with Jacksonians accusing Adams of widespread corruption, most of which charges did not stand up to close scrutiny. Jackson won, and Adams went back to Massachusetts, intending to spend time with farming and reading. Supporters persuaded him to run for Congress in 1830, which he did with success, serving from 1831 to 1848. Among his accomplishments in Congress was helping with the repeal of the 1836 "gag rule" mandating that any petitions against slavery be automatically tabled. In 1848 he had a stroke on the House floor, dying two days later, on February 23.

Andrew Jackson

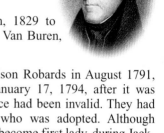

March 15, 1767 – June 8, 1845

Political party: Democratic

Vice president: John C. Calhoun, 1829 to 1832; none 1832 to 1833; Martin Van Buren, 1833 to 1837

First lady: Married Rachel Donelson Robards in August 1791, and in a second ceremony on January 17, 1794, after it was learned that Rachel's earlier divorce had been invalid. They had one child, Andrew Jackson Jr., who was adopted. Although Rachel did not live long enough to become first lady, during Jackson's tenure Rachel's niece Emily Donelson lived at the White House with her husband and served as hostess.

Especially remembered for: Greatest plurality of popular votes gained by any president to date. "The Union must and shall be preserved" statement during the political conflict with Senator John C. Calhoun. Veto of the charter renewal for the 2nd Bank of the United States and his conflict with backers of the Bank. "Kitchen Cabinet" of political cronies. Great prosperity during the early 1830s, including a Treasury surplus. Construction and occupation of the second Philadelphia Mint. Nickname: "Old Hickory."

Andrew Jackson was born in Waxhaw, Carolina, son of Andrew and Elizabeth Hutchinson Jackson. His education was intermittent, causing many later critics to call him illiterate. No matter; he read law for about two years, then entered practice in Tennessee, where he was viewed as very competent. He became well-to-do and built a mansion, Hermitage, near Nashville, and was a slave owner. He was a ready debater, and quickly rose to challenges. In a duel with a man who had insulted his wife, Jackson was the winner.

In 1796 and 1797 Jackson served as a congressman, then as a senator for the next two years, followed by a judicial position on the Tennessee Supreme Court until 1804. As a major general in the War of 1812 he became known as the "Hero of New Orleans." In January 1815 his forces devastated a large corps of British soldiers—even though, unbeknownst to the combatants, the war had ended by a peace settlement in December 1814. He was appointed governor of the newly acquired Florida Territory in 1821, and served as a United States senator from 1823 to 1825.

Jackson giving his "The federal Union—it must be preserved" toast in 1830. (from a painting by C.W. Jefferys)

In 1824 Andrew Jackson ran for president, but lost to John Quincy Adams. In 1828 the two squared off again in a particularly vitriolic contest. Jackson won, and went to the White House, where the doors were opened to everyday citizens—much to the dismay of certain elements of Washington society, who considered the new president to be without finesse or manners. The country became very polarized, with Democrats following Jackson's every step, while the National Republicans or Whigs opposed just about everything he did. A major clash arose with Senator John C. Calhoun and the state of South Carolina, which threatened to nullify federal import tariffs and was considering seceding from the Union. A compromise was negotiated by Henry Clay.

In 1832 the main contender in Jackson's bid for reelection was Clay. At the polls Jackson overwhelmed him with 56% of the popular vote and nearly five times as many Electoral College votes. Jackson had opposed the Second Bank of the United States, a private corporation in which the federal government held a stake and dictated much policy. The charter, up for renewal in 1836, was brought before Congress in 1832 and passed, only to be vetoed by Jackson. This caused a great uproar, as did his moving federal funds to selected state institutions, called "pet banks" by his opponents. In the meantime, the economy experienced great prosperity from development of the West and the sale of public lands, as well as expansion of railroads, canals, and domestic works. The Treasury had a surplus in 1835 and returned money to each state.

After his presidency, Jackson retired to the Hermitage, where he died in 1845.

Hard Times token, circa 1837, satirizing Andrew Jackson. Emerging from a safe, the president is shown holding the nation's money, instead of the second Bank of the United States. The initials LL.D. on the punning jackass image reflect an honorary degree given to him by Harvard, ridiculed by his opponents, as he had no advanced education. (Actual size 26 mm)

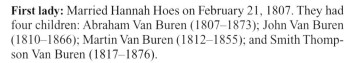

Martin Van Buren

December 5, 1782 – July 24, 1862

Political party: Democratic

Vice president: Richard M. Johnson, 1837 to 1841

First lady: Married Hannah Hoes on February 21, 1807. They had four children: Abraham Van Buren (1807–1873); John Van Buren (1810–1866); Martin Van Buren (1812–1855); and Smith Thompson Van Buren (1817–1876).

Especially remembered for: His loyalty to President Jackson while serving as secretary of state and as vice president. The Panic of 1837, an economic disaster that occurred under his watch. Lack of popularity throughout his presidency.

Martin Van Buren was born in Kinderhook, New York, to Abraham and Maria Hoes Van Buren. He completed his education in 1796 with a degree from Kinderhook Academy. He entered law and became involved in state politics in nearby Albany. As a favorite of the political organization, Van Buren dispensed patronage in a manner intended to generate loyalty and votes. He went up the ladder as a state senator (1813 to 1815), state attorney general (1815 to 1819), United States senator (1821 to 1829), governor of New York state (1829), secretary of state under Jackson (1829 to 1831), minister to England (1831), and vice president (1833 to 1837).

Andrew Jackson's cabinet became dysfunctional in his first term when certain men appointed through John C. Calhoun's recommendations became disloyal to the president's interests. Subsequently Jackson relied on unofficial advisors (his "Kitchen Cabinet," so called because they were said to meet in the White House kitchen). Through this, Secretary of State Van Buren remained a staunch supporter and was rewarded with an ambassadorship to England, after which he became vice president.

Although the Jackson administration had been one of great prosperity, storm clouds gathered in the summer of 1836 when Jackson issued the Specie Circular, seeking to bridle speculation in Western land by making purchases payable only in gold or silver coins, instead of paper money and debt instruments. Riding on Jackson's coattails and the still strong economy, Van Buren was elected president in 1836.

Soon, the economy experienced problems, and there was a tightening of credit. In May 1837, two months after Van Buren's inauguration, most banks suspended payment of silver and gold coins in exchange for paper money. The Hard Times era was on, and

A token satirizing Martin Van Buren, issued in 1840.

did not end until after he left the White House. Thousands of businesses and hundreds of banks closed their doors. During this time many people privately issued copper tokens ridiculing Jackson, Van Buren, or both.

Van Buren was defeated in the 1840 election. In 1848 he ran again, on the new Free Soil Ticket, and lost. He died in Kinderhook in 1862.

William Henry Harrison

February 9, 1773 – April 4, 1841

Political party: Whig

Vice president: John Tyler, 1841

First lady: Married Anna Tuthill Symmes on November 25, 1795. They had 10 children: Elizabeth Bassett Harrison (1796–1846); John Cleves Symmes Harrison (1798–1830); Lucy Singleton Harrison (1800–1826); William Henry Harrison (1802–1838); John Scott Harrison (1804–1878; whose son Benjamin served as president, 1889–1893); Benjamin Harrison (1806–1840); Mary Symmes Harrison (1809–1842); Carter Bassett Harrison (1811–1839); Anna Tuthill Harrison (1813–1865); and James Findlay Harrison (1814–1817).

Especially remembered for: Victor at the Battle of Tippecanoe against fractious Native Americans in 1811. First president to die in office. Shortest presidential term (one month). Nickname: "Old Tippecanoe." The campaign slogan "Tippecanoe and Tyler too."

William Henry Harrison was born in Berkeley, Virginia, son of Benjamin and Elizabeth Bassett Harrison. He took courses in history and classics at Hampden-Sydney College, and then in 1791 began the study of medicine in Richmond. He quickly had a change of heart, and decided to enter the military. Obtaining a commission as an ensign in the First Infantry of the Army, he went to the Western frontier in the prairie states.

Resigning from the Army in 1798, Harrison was appointed as secretary of the Northwest Territory and served as its first delegate to Congress. He was important in legislation to separate the Indiana Territory from the district. Named as governor of Indiana in 1801, he sought to obtain title to Indian land so that settlers from the eastern states could set up homesteads and so that those already living in the area could have peace of mind. The landowners would have none of this, and it fell to Harrison to attack the confederacy formed by the Indians under Chief Tecumseh and his religiously oriented brother, the Prophet. As the settlers became increasingly endangered, Harrison received permission to attack. The Indians struck first, at the Army camp on the Tippecanoe River, before daybreak on November 7, 1811. Harrison was the victor, but with 190 casualties. His routing of the Native Americans was widely hailed as a triumph. He remained governor until 1813. In the War of 1812 he was given the command of the Army in the Northwest, where he vanquished British forces and their Indian allies, killing Tecumseh. From 1816 to 1819 he was a congressman from Ohio, then a United States sena-

Campaign advertisement for Harrison, *The Spirit of '76,* **May 9, 1840, inviting Indiana men to come to "the field of Tippecanoe" for a rally on May 29.**

tor from the same state (1825 to 1828), then minister to Columbia in 1828 and 1829.

Harrison went back to civilian life, but in 1840 answered the call of the Whig party as nominee for president. The campaign, with Harrison and Tyler (as vice president), featured "Tippecanoe and Tyler too" against incumbent Martin Van Buren. Harrison won by a popular plurality of less than 150,000 votes, but carried the day in the Electoral College with 234 votes to Van Buren's 60. In March 1841 his inaugural address, edited by Daniel Webster, had elegant touches of the classic and promised to advance the cause of the average citizen. Unfortunately he became chilled, caught pneumonia, and died on April 4.

William H. Harrison campaign medal of 1840 with "the log cabin candidate" motif and inscription.

John Tyler

March 29, 1790 – January 18, 1862

Political party: Whig

Vice president: None

First lady: Married Letitia Christian, on March 29, 1813; his second wife was Julia Gardiner, whom he married on June 26, 1844. They had 15 children: Mary Tyler (1815–1848); Robert Tyler (1816–1877); John Tyler (1819–1896); Letitia Tyler (1821–1907); Elizabeth Tyler (1823–1850); Anne Contesse Tyler (1825); Alice Tyler (1827–1854); Tazewell Tyler (1830–1874); David Gardiner Tyler (1846–1927); John Alexander Tyler (1848–1883); Julia Gardiner Tyler (1849–1871); Lachlan Tyler (1851–1902); Lyon Gardiner Tyler (1853–1935); Robert Fitzwalter Tyler (1856–1927); and Pearl Tyler (1860–1947).

Especially remembered for: Being the first vice president to be elevated to the office of president by the death of his predecessor—the "accidental president," as some opponents nicknamed him.

John Tyler was born in Greenway, Virginia, son of John and Mary Marot Armistead Tyler. He graduated from the College of William and Mary in 1807. He practiced law and became involved in politics, included as a congressman from 1816 to 1821, Virginia state legislator (1823 to 1835) and governor (1825 and 1826), and United States senator (1827 to 1836). An early supporter of Jackson, Tyler changed his philosophy and took up the advocacy of states' rights, with less power to the federal government.

Although in the 1840 contest Tyler took up the "Tippecanoe and Tyler too" banner, he felt that the slogan was nationalistic. Henry Clay and Daniel Webster carried considerable weight with newly elected president William Henry Harrison. After Harrison's unexpected death, Clay and Webster believed that Tyler would encompass their ideas as well. This did not happen, and in a pivotal move Tyler vetoed a new plan for a national bank brought forward by Clay. Matters went from bad to worse, and the entire Cabinet, inherited from Harrison, resigned save for Secretary of State Webster. Tyler was ejected from the Whig party, which controlled Congress. The first impeachment bill against a president was introduced into the House of Representatives after he vetoed a tariff bill, but failed.

States' rights advocacy was the rallying call of the South, and relations between North and South were strained under Tyler. Despite political problems, his administration had several achievements, including an act to enable settlers to take possession of 160 acres of public land for farming before it was put up for public sale. The Webster-Ashburton Treaty resolved a border dispute with Canada. In 1842 a protective tariff bill aided Northern manufacturers and helped speed the end of the Hard Times era. In 1845 Texas was annexed by the Union.

After South Carolina seceded from the Union in December 1860, followed by other Southern states, Tyler helped form the government of the Confederate States of America. He died in 1862, in the Confederate capital of Richmond, while a member of the Confederate House of Representatives.

James Knox Polk

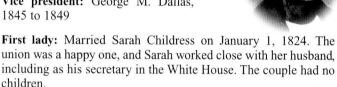

November 2, 1795 – June 15, 1849

Political party: Democratic

Vice president: George M. Dallas, 1845 to 1849

First lady: Married Sarah Childress on January 1, 1824. The union was a happy one, and Sarah worked close with her husband, including as his secretary in the White House. The couple had no children.

Especially remembered for: His dynamic administration included expansion of the boundaries of the United States, reflecting imperialism and also adding acrimony to the long-standing differences between the North and the South concerning slavery in new states. The War with Mexico. New boundaries for the Oregon Territory. The beginning of the California Gold Rush. During Polk's administration, dancing and drinking were not allowed in the White House, in observance of Mrs. Polk's religious convictions.

James Knox Polk was born in Mecklenburg County, North Carolina, the son of Samuel and Jane Knox Polk. In 1818 he graduated with honors from the University of North Carolina, after which he practiced law. He soon became absorbed in politics, became a friend of Andrew Jackson, and ran for public office. From 1823 to 1825 he was a state representative, then a representative to the United States Congress from 1825 to 1839, serving as speaker from 1835 onward. During the early part of the decade he supported Jackson in his conflict with the second Bank of the United States. Afterward he was governor of Tennessee from 1829 to 1841.

In 1844 he was considered to be a strong possibility for vice president, with Martin Buren expected to get the nod for president at the Democratic nominating convention. Polk aired his expansionist views, stating that Texas, California, and the Oregon Territory should come under federal control, upstaging what the earlier defeated (in 1840) Van Buren had to offer. Jackson admired Polk's views as a part of the "manifest destiny" to enlarge the United States, and influenced attendees to nominate him as president, which happened on the ninth ballot. In the general election in November he beat Henry Clay, the Whig candidate.

Prior to Polk's inauguration, both houses of Congress offered Texas the opportunity to be annexed to the United States, risking a clash with Mexico. In office, the president intimidated and negotiated with England to secure much of the Oregon Territory, defining what became the southern border of Canada. To secure California, Polk sent an envoy to Mexico with an offer of $20 million plus cancellation of damage claims owed. The thought of selling such a vast territory was not interesting to the authorities to the south, and they declined to discuss the matter. To force attention, Polk sent General Zachary Taylor and

Portrait of James Knox Polk from a Bureau of Engraving and Printing vignette book, 1876.

troops to the Rio Grande area. This was perceived by the Mexicans as aggression, and they attacked the American forces. Thus was launched the war with Mexico of 1846 and 1847. Mexico acknowledged defeat after a series of decisive battles. California and New Mexico were ceded to the United States for $15 million and settlement of damage claims. Soon afterward, on January 24, 1848, nuggets were found in the American River at Sutter's mill, in California, launching the Gold Rush.

The acquisition of the vast new districts precipitated bitter arguments in Congress as to whether new states and territories should permit slavery. In the next decade this would become the main focus of debates in the nation's capital, while differences between the North and the South continued to widen. After he left the White House, Polk went back to Tennessee, where in poor health he died a few months later on June 15, 1849.

A government act of March 3, 1849, authorized a new coin: the large $20 gold "double eagle," containing almost a full ounce of precious metal.

Zachary Taylor

November 24, 1784 – July 9, 1850

Political party: Whig

Vice president: Millard Fillmore, 1849 and 1850

First lady: Married Margaret Mackall Smith on June 21, 1810. In the White House Margaret was ill much of the time and did not attend most functions. The couple had six children: Ann Mackall Taylor (1811–1875); Sarah Knox Taylor (1814–1835); Octavia P. Taylor (1816–1820); Margaret Smith Taylor (1819–1820); Mary Elizabeth Taylor (1824–1909); and Richard Taylor (1826–1879).

Especially remembered for: As the hero of the War with Mexico he was admired by both the North and the South, while Southerners appreciated him as an owner of slaves. His brief presidency did not accomplish much in the way of national progress. Nickname: "Old Rough and Ready."

Zachary Taylor was born near Barboursville, Virginia, son of Lieutenant Colonel Richard and Sarah Dabney Strother Taylor. He was a second cousin of James Madison. Zachary spent his youth on a plantation in Kentucky. With but a meager formal education he followed a military career while maintaining his own plantation in Mississippi, complete with a large retinue of slaves to plant and pick cotton. Taylor had no advanced schooling. In the Army he gained fame by vanquishing pesky Indians. In the war with Mexico, he shared heroic honors with General Winfield Scott. Taylor had little interest in politics, and never voted in a presidential election.

For the contest of 1848 the Whigs nominated Taylor, while the choice of the Democrats was Lewis Cass. In protest against both Taylor holding slaves and Cass wanting to allow states to decide for themselves if they wanted slavery, the Free Soil Party became strong in the North and posted Van Buren. The latter took votes away from Cass, propelling Taylor into the White House, although he had not campaigned actively.

America continued to be torn by the slavery question. Taylor suggested that the territories of California and New Mexico (including what is today Arizona) draft their own constitutions and apply for statehood, making their own provisions regarding the issue. Southern politicians were incensed, claiming that it was the right of Congress to determine the status of slaves. Some threatened secession. Taylor was firm, stating in 1850 that if need be he would personally command the Army

Portrait of Zachary Taylor from a Bureau of Engraving and Printing vignette book, 1876.

in the suppression of such a notion. Ironically, in the Civil War a decade later his only son Richard was appointed as a general in the army of the Confederate States of America.

Unforeseen events intervened when Taylor became ill on July 4, 1850, in ceremonies at the Washington Monument (under construction since 1836, with work dragging on until 1888). He died a few days later on July 9. Vice President Millard Fillmore succeeded him as chief executive.

Millard Fillmore

January 7, 1800 – March 8, 1874

Political party: Whig

Vice president: None

First lady: Married Abigail Powers on February 5, 1826. The union was blissful. The couple had two children: Millard Powers Fillmore (1828–1889); and Mary Abigail Fillmore (1832–1854). His second wife was Caroline Carmichael McIntosh, a wealthy widow whom he married on February 10, 1858.

Especially remembered for: Debates over the Compromise of 1850, which he favored. Signing the unfortunate Fugitive Slave Act. Good economy fueled by the Gold Rush. The slavery question dominated Fillmore's administration, as it would his successors'. He was faithful to his duties and trust, but undistinguished in the annals of the presidency.

Millard Fillmore was born in Locke Township, Cayuga County, New York, son of Nathaniel and Phoebe Millard Fillmore. He grew up on the family farm in what was at the time part of the western frontier. His early education was sparse, and at the age of 15 he was apprenticed to a wool carder. Imbued with ambition, he pursued further studies when he was 19 years old, read law, and in 1823 was admitted to the bar. In 1830 he set up his office in Buffalo, by which time he had been a member of the New York State Assembly for two years, then continuing to 1831. Well-known politician Thurlow Weed was a friend and mentor. From 1833 to 1835 and again from 1837 to 1845 Fillmore served in the United States House of Representatives. In 1848 he was the comptroller of the state of New York when he joined Zachary Taylor as running mate on the Whig ticket.

When Fillmore unexpectedly became president after Taylor's death, the question of slavery in the new territories was still being fiercely debated in the halls of Congress—again, the North against the South. Taylor's Cabinet resigned, and Fillmore filled the vacancies with his own choices, including Daniel Webster as secretary of state. Under Senator Stephen A. Douglas, the Compromise of 1850 was worked out, providing that California be admitted to the Union as a free state, slavery be abolished in the District of Columbia, boundary disputes between Texas and New Mexico be resolved, and slaveholders be given the right to pursue and capture escaped slaves in the North (the Fugitive Slave Act).

Portrait of Millard Fillmore from a Bureau of Engraving and Printing vignette book, 1876.

The Whig party became ineffective as many Northerners would not forgive Fillmore for not vetoing the Fugitive Slave Act. The plight of Southern slaves loomed worse than ever. In 1856 Fillmore was invited to become a part of the newly formed Republican Party, but declined, and became the presidential candidate for the American or, more popularly, the "Know Nothing" Party. This bid failed, and Fillmore left public service.

In later years he was a critic of President Abraham Lincoln, but during Reconstruction supported President Johnson. Fillmore died in Buffalo, New York, in 1874.

Franklin Pierce

November 23, 1804 – October 8, 1869

Political party: Democratic

Vice president: William King, 1853; none 1853 to 1857

First lady: Married Jane Means Appleton on November 10, 1834. The couple had three children: Franklin Pierce (1836; died when three days old); Frank Robert Pierce (1839–1843); and Benjamin Pierce (1841–1853). Two months before he took office, he and his wife saw 11-year-old Benjamin killed when their train was wrecked. Jane dressed in black thereafter, and as first lady was consumed with grief and delusions, including writing letters to her dead son.

Especially remembered for: Being undistinguished as a leader—a minor presidential figure, as were his two predecessors. The continuation of Gold Rush prosperity.

Franklin Pierce was born in Hillsborough, New Hampshire, son of General Benjamin Pierce and Ann Kendrick Pierce. In 1824 he graduated from Bowdoin College, after which he studied law, then entered the political arena. At the age of 24 he was elected to the New Hampshire Legislature, becoming speaker of that body two years later. Then followed service in the United States House of Representatives from 1833 to 1837, then in the Senate from 1837 to 1842. He then returned to New Hampshire, as his wife Jane disliked living in Washington and the couple had suffered the loss of an infant son (in 1836). Later, Pierce served in the war with Mexico.

In 1852 at the Democratic convention the delegates decided upon a platform to support the Compromise of 1850 and to resist any further stirring of the slavery question, which by this time had dominated American politics for many years and had rendered ineffective the two most recent presidents (Taylor and Fillmore). There was no unanimity on a nominee for president, and after an exhausting 48 ballots Pierce was selected, one of the most obscure "dark horse" candidates ever.

Elected that November, Pierce in his inaugural address in March 1853 promised an era of peace and prosperity. Moving into the White House was a somber event, as he and his wife had suffered the loss of another son, Benjamin, in a train accident two months earlier. There were few festivities and no inaugural ball.

Despite continuing animosity between the North and the South, the economy had been sound since the end of the Hard Times era in 1843, and was still growing. Railroads were a particularly dynamic part of the equation. Soon the new president was viewed with suspicion by many Northerners, who felt he was soft on slavery and was working for the interests of the South. His administration was wracked by this continuing question, which came to a head with the Kansas-Nebraska Act, engineered by Senator Stephen A. Douglas, which repealed the Missouri Compromise of 1820 and threw open the possibility of slavery beyond the boundaries of that state. Douglas was an advocate of building railroads in the West and sought to organize governments in the districts through which the main line toward California would run. The $10-million Gadsden Purchase of land from Mexico (at the southern border of New Mexico) was made to facilitate the route. Douglas felt that citizens of the Western areas should decide the slavery question for themselves. "Bleeding Kansas" saw widespread destruction and killing as renegades from both the North and the South rushed there to gain control.

After his presidency, Pierce returned to his native state. His wife died in 1863, after which alcohol became his companion. He died of cirrhosis of the liver in Concord, New Hampshire, in 1869.

James Buchanan

April 23, 1791 – June 1, 1868

Political party: Democratic

Vice president: John C. Breckinridge, 1857 to 1861

Marital status: The only president never to marry; he had been engaged earlier at age 28, but his fiancée committed suicide. A niece, Harriet Lane (1830–1904), orphaned at age 11 and his ward since that time, served as hostess at the White House.

Especially remembered for: Trying to appease both the North and the South and pleasing neither. Known as "Old Buck," he pronounced his name similar to *buck-cannon*; indeed both items were shown on an 1856 campaign medal.

James Buchanan was born in Cove Gap, Pennsylvania, son of James and Elizabeth Speer Buchanan. Scion of a prosperous family, he was raised with the trappings of the good life. In 1809 he graduated from Dickinson College. Buchanan was well studied in law and a talented debater. He went from one success to another. He gravitated into politics as state representative in 1815 and 1816, then as a United States congressman from 1821 to 1821, minister to Russia (1832 to 1834), and United States senator (1834 to 1845). Under James Knox Polk he was secretary of state from 1845 to 1849, then minister to England for most of the Pierce administration from 1853 to 1856.

In 1856 Buchanan was the choice for president on the Democratic ticket. Having been overseas in recent years, he was unscarred by controversy over the slavery question. The fourth time was a charm, as he had sought the nod unsuccessfully in 1844, 1848, and 1852. He was elected handily in a three-way contest with Millard Fillmore and John C. Frémont, and in March 1857 went to the White House. In his inaugural address he dismissed the question of slavery in the territories, stating that the Supreme Court would soon decide the matter. Then, two days later, Chief Justice Roger B. Taney ruled that Congress had no power to deprive holders of slaves in the territories of their right of ownership. Northerners were outraged, while Southerners rejoiced. Buchanan was aware of worsening differences between the North and the South, and sought to quiet the matter by making Cabinet and other appointments from both sides, with his bias toward the South being obvious.

Portrait of James Buchanan from a Bureau of Engraving and Printing vignette book, 1876.

To stop the conflict in "Bloody Kansas" he recommended that the district be admitted as a slave state, which turned some members of his own Democratic party against him, although many members were oriented toward Southern views. The matter was set aside, and statehood would not occur until years later. The Panic of 1857 caused wide financial hardship from autumn of that year through 1858. In the latter year the House was under Republican control and Democrats ruled the Senate. Neither party would support the other, and much legislation reached an impasse.

The Democrats divided into Northern and Southern factions, strengthening the position of the Republicans. Buchanan did not seek a second term. When Abraham Lincoln won the presidential election of November 1860, tempers broke loose in the South. South Carolina seceded on December 20, followed in early 1861 by the formation of the Confederate States of America. The Buchanan administration, never strong to begin with, fell into shambles as many key appointees and other government officials left Washington and joined the Confederacy.

In March 1861 Buchanan left the capital and when to his mansion, Wheatland, near Lancaster, Pennsylvania. He died in 1868.

The "Indian Head" cent was introduced during James Buchanan's presidency, in 1859. It actually depicts a symbolic Miss Liberty wearing an Indian headdress, not an actual Native American.

Abraham Lincoln

February 12, 1809 – April 15, 1865

Political party: Republican

Vice president: Hannibal Hamlin, 1861 to 1865; Andrew Johnson, 1865

First lady: Married Mary Todd on November 4, 1842. The couple had four boys (only one of whom lived to maturity): Robert Todd Lincoln (1843–1926); Edward Baker Lincoln (1846–1850); William Wallace Lincoln (1850–1862); and Thomas "Tad" Lincoln (1853–1871).

Especially remembered for: "Log cabin" childhood. Illinois rail-splitter. Leadership in the Civil War. Emancipation Proclamation. Viewed as a hero by the North, a scoundrel by the South. Assassination. Nicknames: "Honest Abe," "the Great Emancipator." One of four presidents honored on Mount Rushmore.

Abraham Lincoln was born on February 12, 1809, in Hodgenville, Kentucky, son of Thomas and Nancy Hanks Lincoln. He grew up in the semi-wilderness of the frontier, where his family had to work hard, and many efforts were a struggle. When he was eight, he moved with his family to Indiana. When he was ten his mother died, and in time he gained a stepmother, Sarah Bush Johnston Lincoln. With ambition and perseverance young Abe gained an education largely on his own, learning to read, write, and do mathematics. He worked hard on a farm, split rails to make fences, and kept a store in New Salem, Illinois, his adopted state.

Lincoln was a captain in the Black Hawk War, after which he practiced law, riding the circuit of courts in his district. Elected in

1834, for eight years he served in the Illinois State Legislature. In 1847 and 1849 he was a representative to Congress. In 1858 he opposed Stephen A. Douglas in the race for the national Senate, and lost. His debates in that contest gained national attention and brought him the fame that secured the Republican nomination for president in 1860. With four candidates running and with the Democrats divided into North–South factions, Lincoln won the November election.

His stance against slavery was intolerable to the South, and in December the state of South Carolina seceded from the Union, followed by six others which soon formed the Confederate States of America. When Lincoln was inaugurated in March 1861, the government was in disarray. Precipitated by the Confederate shelling of federal Fort Sumter in the Charleston, South Carolina, harbor on April 11 and its evacuation, war was declared against the South on April 15. It was expected to be of short duration, as Lincoln and others felt

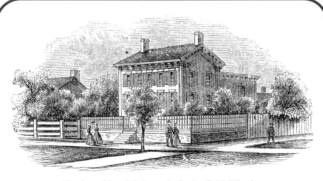

Abraham Lincoln's home in Springfield, Illinois.
(Lossing, *Pictorial Field Book of the Civil War*, 1874)

the Confederacy was ill prepared with resources. The president called for three-month enlistments from volunteer soldiers. Reality proved to be vastly different, and the Civil War lasted until early April 1865.

Lincoln was faced with reorganizing many departments in the government, supervising the Army and Navy, financing the war, and dealing with disarray in the monetary system. On January 1, 1863, he issued the Emancipation Proclamation, freeing slaves in the Confederacy, which had little practical effect until the war was over. In 1864 he won reelection against his opponent, General George B. McClellan, who he had relieved of his Army command due to perceived poor performance.

Less than a week after the war ended (on April 9, 1865), President Lincoln was shot while attended a performance at Ford's Theatre in Washington. He was rushed to a nearby boarding house, and died in the early hours of April 15. During his tenure the country had known less than six weeks of peace. He was succeeded in the White House by his vice president, Andrew Johnson.

1918 Illinois Centennial commemorative half dollar with a strong, contemplative portrait of Lincoln.

Andrew Johnson

December 29, 1808 – July 31, 1875

Political party: Democratic

Vice president: None

First lady: Married Eliza McCardle on May 5, 1827.
The couple had five children: Martha Johnson (1828–1901); Charles Johnson (1830–1863); Mary Johnson (1832–1883); Robert Johnson (1834–1869); and Andrew Johnson (1852–1879).

Especially remembered for: Efforts at reconstruction of the South after the Civil War. Impeachment and acquittal. The purchase of Alaska from Russia.

Andrew Johnson was born in Raleigh, North Carolina, son of Jacob and Mary McDonough Johnson, who struggled in poverty. Young Andrew never attended school, but as a child was apprenticed to a tailor. He fled, in time opening his own tailor shop in Greeneville, Tennessee. For the rest of his life he made most of his own clothes. He learned to read and write through instruction from his wife Eliza, and at the local academy was recognized for his talents as a debater. Entering politics, he became an alderman in Greeneville in 1830 and was elected mayor in 1834. From there it was to the Tennessee State Legislature from 1835 to 1843, then to the United States House of Representatives from 1843 to 1853. In the House he championed the rights of poor people and supported legislation to provide farms to people who would work on and manage them.

Next, he served as governor of his state to 1857, then as a United States senator to 1862. From the latter year to 1865 he remained in the Senate, although Tennessee had seceded. This made him a traitor in the view of most Southerners and a hero to Northerners. At the 1864 Republican nominating convention, the party stated that it welcomed all loyal men regardless of prior political affiliation. Johnson, although both a Southerner and Democrat, was selected as the candidate for vice president, running with Lincoln.

After Lincoln's death, Johnson moved quickly into the complex problems of the presidency in the aftermath of the Civil War. Although Congress was not in session and would not be until December, he set about reconstructing the Union. An automatic pardon was given to all who would swear to an oath of allegiance, except former leaders and wealthy supporters of the Confederacy, who had to apply for a presidential pardon.

When Congress convened, there was much debate and dissention about the condition of the South. Many of Johnson's moves were criticized. Matters were not going well in many districts, as former leaders during the Confederacy were holding new offices, and although blacks were legally free, many restrictions were made to regulate them. Clearly, many Southerners did not want to see black Americans achieve the same status as whites, or to hold elective office.

Scene in Ford's Theatre on the evening of April 14, 1865, moments after John Wilkes Booth (fleeing to the left) shot President Lincoln (in the box above the right side of the stage). (*Harper's Weekly,* April 29, 1865)

Congress refused to seat any representative or senator who had held a significant office in the Confederacy. Rights of blacks were enhanced, at least in theory, with the Civil Rights Act of 1866 and with the 14th amendment to the Constitution, which provided that no state could "deprive any person of life, liberty, or property, without due process of law." In the South, all state legislatures except Tennessee refused to ratify the amendment.

In March 1867, Congress took reconstruction efforts a step further and placed Southern states under military rule and set up restrictions on the president's actions. When Johnson dismissed Secretary of War Edwin M. Stanton, he was accused of violating the Tenure of Office Act. The House of Representatives voted 11 impeachment articles against him. The matter went to the Senate in spring 1868, where he was acquitted by a single vote.

Throughout Johnson's term, ending in March 1869, reconstruction had been very difficult. The smooth transition of former slaves into society had seen many setbacks, caused in no small part by Congress resisting many of the president's policies.

In 1875, Andrew Johnson returned to the United States Senate—a vindication of his career by citizens of his state— but served only briefly before dying that summer in Carter's Station, Tennessee.

Portrait of Andrew Johnson from a Bureau of Engraving and Printing vignette book, 1876.

Ulysses S. Grant

April 27, 1822 – July 23, 1885

Political party: Republican

Vice president: Schuyler Colfax, 1869 to 1873; Henry Wilson, 1873 to 1875; none 1875 to 1877

First lady: Married Julia Boggs Dent on August 22, 1848. The couple had four children: Frederick Dent Grant (1850–1912); Ulysses Simpson Grant (1852–1929); Ellen Wrenshall Grant (1855–1922); and Jesse Root Grant (1858–1934).

Especially remembered for: Military service during the Civil War. Being a great general but a below-average president. Allowing himself to be used by others. Depiction on several types of paper money (most famously the $50 bill) and on commemorative coins.

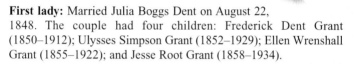

U.S. Grant (as he was generally known) was born in Point Pleasant, Ohio, son of Jesse Root and Hannah Simpson Grant. His father was a tanner, and the family was of average financial circumstances. He was sent to West Point against his preference, his father insisting on the matter, where he graduated near the bottom of his class. He received an Army commission and embarked on a military career, but resigned (according to some rumors, after being caught drinking on duty).

At the outset of the Civil War in the spring of 1861, Grant was clerking for his father in a leather shop in Galena, Illinois. He was tapped by the governor to head a disorganized regiment of volunteer soldiers. He performed with distinction, turning the unit into a dynamic company. This was recognized, and by September 1861 he was a brigadier general.

Grant was sent to gain federal control of the Mississippi River. In February 1862 he captured Fort Henry and mounted an attack against Fort Donelson. The Confederate general in charge asked for terms to be negotiated, to which Grant replied that the only option was unconditional surrender. President Lincoln advanced Grant to major general. At the Battle of Shiloh he suffered a setback, and some suggested that Lincoln remove him from command. The president kept his faith in Grant. He went on to take Vicksburg, Mississippi, after a long and bitter siege, thus dividing the Confederacy into two parts. From there he vanquished the Confederates at Chattanooga. Lincoln appointed him as general–in–chief in March. Grant directed much of the rest of the war, including sending General William Tecumseh Sherman on this march through Georgia and the South, and the defeat of General Robert E. Lee's Army of Northern Virginia. On April 9, 1865, General Lee surrendered at Appomattox Court House in Virginia. Grant formulated terms that prevented treason trials and were intended to smooth the return of Confederate soldiers to civilian life.

Standing portrait of U.S. Grant.
(*John Sherman's Recollections*)

As a military hero he was swept into the presidency in the 1868 election. Citizens hoped that the turmoil of Reconstruction under the Johnson administration would come to a satisfactory conclusion. This did not happen. Grant seemed to be overwhelmed with the intricacies of the government and the problems confronting it. Unwisely, he accepted gifts from those seeking government favors. In one memorable gaffe he warmly met two notorious stock-market speculators and manipulators, James Fisk and Jay Gould, who later conspired to corner the market in gold.

Despite many problems, including alcoholism, Grant persevered, and in the 1872 presidential contest he was reelected. His second term ran its course without distinction, as Reconstruction problems continued, with many eventually worked out through actions in the South, not by presidential leadership.

After he left office in 1877 he joined a financial firm as a partner. The company went bankrupt. In desperate financial straits and with cancer of the throat, Grant began to write his memoirs. The project was completed shortly before his death at a resort in Mount Gregor, New York, on July 23, 1885. After publication, the book became a bestseller and earned his family nearly $450,000.

Grant's boyhood home in Point Pleasant, Ohio, as it appeared in an 1885 photograph (*Century Magazine,* October 1885) and on the reverse of the 1922 Grant Centennial commemorative half dollar.

Rutherford B. Hayes

October 4, 1822 – January 17, 1893

Political party: Republican

Vice president: William Wheeler, 1877 to 1881

First lady: Married Lucy Ware Webb on December 30, 1852. The couple had eight children: Birchard Austin Hayes (1853–1926); James Webb Cook Hayes (1856–1934); Rutherford Platt Hayes (1858–1927); Joseph Thompson Hayes (1861–1863); George Crook Hayes (1864–1866); Fanny Hayes (1867–1950); Scott Russell Hayes (1871–1923); and Manning Force Hayes (1873–1874). In the White House the first lady was known as Lemonade Lucy, as she forbid the serving of alcohol.

Especially remembered for: The most contested, controversial election results up to that time in history. Integrity and temperance, seemingly a contrast to the previous administration. Presidency marked by lack of cooperation between Northern and Southern factions.

Rutherford B. Hayes was born in Delaware, Ohio, to Rutherford and Sophia Birchard Hayes. He graduated from Kenyon College in 1842 and Harvard Law School in 1845, after which he practiced law for five years in Lower Sandusky, Ohio, then went to Cincinnati where he continued in the profession and also became involved in politics in the Whig party. Hayes served in the Civil War, rose to become brevet major general, and was wounded in action. Afterward he went to the United States House of Representatives from 1865 to 1867, where he was disturbed at the direction Reconstruction had taken, and felt that the Johnson administration was overly influenced by former Confederates. He then served terms as governor of his home state from 1868 to 1872 and again in 1876 and 1877.

In 1876 Hayes was nominated as the Republican candidate for president, opposing Samuel J. Tilden, governor of New York State. Although Hayes had many supporters—Mark Twain among them—he had no illusions of victory. After the popular votes were counted, the score was 4,300,000 for Tilden and just 4,036,000 for Hayes. At the Electoral College, votes from Florida, Louisiana, and South Carolina were disputed. Tilden would be the winner if just one of these votes went to him, but for Hayes to be elected he would need all in contention. The matter was hotly disputed. In January 1877, with no winner declared, Congress established a commission to decide. Made up of eight Republicans and seven Democrats, the vote was down party lines, and every disputed vote was given to Hayes, the final count being 185 to 184.

Hayes endeavored to appoint Cabinet members and other key officials on merit, causing problems with others in his party who had promised or indicated patronage for certain interests in the South, including at least one Cabinet post and the withdrawal of federal troops from Louisiana and South Carolina, in order to gain their support. He did not do this, after which his administration lost influence in that region, weakening its policies. Hayes did not seek reelection, but retired to Spiegel Grove, his estate in Fremont, Ohio, where he lived until his death early in 1893.

President Hayes taking the oath of office at his inauguration.
(*Harper's Weekly,* March 24, 1877)

James A. Garfield

November 19, 1831 – September 19, 1881

Political party: Republican

Vice president: Chester Alan Arthur, 1881

First lady: Married Lucretia Rudolph on November 11, 1858. She was well read in classics, designed the family's mansion, and was a devout adherent to the Disciples of Christ. The couple had seven children: Eliza A. Garfield (1860–1863); Harry A. Garfield (1863–1942); James R. Garfield (1865–1950); Mary Garfield (1867–1947); Irvin M. Garfield (1870–1951); Abram Garfield (1872–1958); and Edward Garfield (1874–1876).

Especially remembered for: Brief presidency terminated by his assassination. The statement, "Whoever controls the volume of money in any country is master of all its legislation and commerce."

James A. Garfield was born in Orange, Ohio, son of Abram and Eliza Ballou Garfield. When James was two years old his father died. As a youth he worked at various occupations including driving mule teams that towed canal boats. In 1856 he graduated from Williams College in Massachusetts. He joined the faculty of the Western Reserve Eclectic Institute (later known as Hiram College) as a professor in the classics, and within a year was named president of the institution.

In 1859 Garfield was elected to the Ohio State Senate on the Republican ticket. In the Civil War he distinguished himself in action in 1862 when he led a brigade against Confederate soldiers at Middle Creek, Kentucky. He was made a brigadier general, and two years later a general. In the meantime, in 1862 he was elected as an Ohio representative to the United States Congress. With the advice of President Lincoln he resigned his commission. For 18 years he was in the House of Representatives, later becoming the leading Republican in that body. Then in 1880 he was elected to the Senate.

For the 1880 nomination Garfield endorsed John Sherman, but the effort was a failure. Finally, on the 36th ballot Garfield himself was chosen, the first truly "dark horse" candidate since Franklin Pierce in 1852. In the popular vote he bested his Democratic opponent (General Winfield Scott Hancock) by just 10,000 votes. After his inauguration, certain of his appointments had to be ratified by the Senate. The spoils went to the victor, and presidents of this era gained many advantages by dispensing patronage. Senator Roscoe Conkling of New York, one of the most powerful men in that legislative body, insisted that many of his favorites be appointed. Garfield complied for most, but a contretemps arose when the president ignored Conkling's preference for the collector of the Port of New York, America's main port of entry. The two sparred, but Garfield secured the necessary votes to confirm his choice.

On July 2, 1881, Charles J. Guiteau, a disappointed office seeker, shot the president in a Washington railroad station. After much suffering punctuated by a brief hope of recovery, Garfield died from internal hemorrhage and infection on September 19, at the New Jersey seaside where he had been taken to rest. He was succeeded by his vice president, Chester Alan Arthur.

The inauguration of James A. Garfield at the front of the U.S. Capitol, 1881.

Chester Alan Arthur

October 5, 1829 – November 18, 1886

Political party: Republican

Vice president: None

Marriage and family: Married Ellen Lewis Herndon (only child of Captain William Lewis Herndon, USN, who went down with the *Central America* in 1857) on October 25, 1859. She died of pneumonia on January 12, 1880. The couple had three children: William Lewis Herndon Arthur (1860–1863); Chester Alan Arthur (1864–1937); and Ellen Herndon Arthur (1871–1915). At the White House his sister Mary (Mrs. John E. McElroy) served as hostess and helped care for his daughter Ellen.

Especially remembered for: The first significant federal immigration law, enacted during his administration. His dislike of the furnishings of the White House; he did not move in until it was redecorated in the Victorian style with everything new. (The old furniture was sold at auction.) Change of his reputation from one of distrust when he became president to respect when he left office.

Chester Alan Arthur was born in Fairfield, Vermont, son of William and Malvina Stone Arthur. His father, who had come to America from Ireland, was a Baptist minister. Chester Arthur graduated from Union College a Phi Beta Kappa in 1848, then taught school while studying law. Admitted to the bar, he practiced law in New York City. After the Civil War commenced he served for a time as quartermaster general for New York State.

In 1871 President U.S. Grant appointed him as collector of the Port of New York, one of the most prized political plums, controlled by Roscoe Conkling and his Republican cronies. He dutifully made his nearly 1,000 employees beholden to Conkling's interests. In 1878, President Rutherford B. Hayes ousted Arthur from the post. As vice president he supported Conkling in his sparring with President Garfield over the latest nomination for this political plum.

When Arthur succeeded to the presidency following the death of Garfield, he took full advantage of dispensing patronage, although without dishonesty. He personally enjoyed the "good life," dressed well, and enjoyed the company of those prominent in society.

In contradiction, he advocated civil service reform. The Pendleton Act of 1883 set up the Civil Service Commission, which prohibited politicians from extracting money from appointees, and made certain positions available to the best-qualified applicants.

A supporter of tariff reform, he advocated lowering rates so that the government would not have surpluses and at the same time imported goods would be cheaper. The effort was partially successful in the Tariff Act of 1883. Arthur worked for a general immigration law that excluded criminals, paupers, and the mentally ill from coming to America. The Chinese Exclusion Act, passed by Congress in 1880, took effect in 1882 and remained in force for 10 years. Prejudice against the Chinese would continue for several decades, and immigrants from China would be referred to as "the yellow peril."

Chester A. Arthur registering to vote in New York City. (*Leslie's Illustrated Newspaper,* October 28, 1882)

By the end of his term Arthur had earned the respect of many legislators and the public. In 1884, he sought reelection on the Republican ticket, although he was suffering from a fatal kidney disease that he had not disclosed to the public. He was not nominated.

Chester Alan Arthur died in New York City in 1886.

Grover Cleveland

March 18, 1837 – June 24, 1908

Political party: Democratic

Vice president: Thomas Hendricks, 1885; none 1885 to 1889

First lady: Married Frances Folsom on June 2, 1886. She was the daughter of his late law partner, and he had been her legal guardian since she was 11. Although he had fathered a child earlier, he did not marry the mother. He was the only president to have his wedding ceremony in the White House. They had five children: Ruth Cleveland (1891–1904); Esther Cleveland (1893–1980); Marion Cleveland (1895–1977); Richard Folsom Cleveland (1897–1974); and Francis Grover Cleveland (1903–1995).

Especially remembered for: Objective evaluation of legislative proposals with a desire to be fair and to benefit the citizenry. Action against scandals involving railroads. Passage of the Interstate Commerce Act.

Grover Cleveland was born in Caldwell, New Jersey, on March 18, 1837, son of Richard Falley Cleveland (a Presbyterian minister) and Anne Neal Cleveland. He was raised in upstate New York with no advanced education, but read law and set up practice in Buffalo.

Cleveland served as sheriff of Erie County, New York, from 1870 to 1873, as mayor of Buffalo on a platform of reform in 1882, and governor of New York from 1883 to 1885. As the Democratic presidential candidate in 1884 he faced Republican James G. Blaine of Maine, nicknamed "the Plumed Knight," and widely considered to be the favorite. The tide turned when a well-meaning supporter of Blaine chastised the Democratic party as one of "rum, Romanism, and rebellion," the "Romanism" referring to members of the Catholic church. This aroused many citizens who had been sitting on the sidelines, who voted for Cleveland, making him the victor. He was the first Democrat to reach the White House since James Buchanan was elected in 1856.

With a dislike of social functions and formal dinners, Cleveland was seemingly a dedicated bachelor. That ended on June 2, 1886, when he took as his bride the 21-year-old Frances Folsom, in a ceremony performed at the White House.

The president endeavored to be impartial to groups seeking to gain influence, and to promote legislation he considered to be in the public good. He aided farmers in Texas crippled by drought, vetoed fraudulent applications for Civil War veterans' pensions, and probed irregularities in the granting of vast tracts of Western land to railroads which had bribed legislators, resulting in 81 million acres being returned to the government. He also endorsed the Interstate Commerce Act, which regulated railroads.

In 1887 Cleveland called for Congress to reduce certain import tariffs that he felt remained unnecessarily high. This angered many Northern supporters, who desired to protect domestic industry. In 1888 he ran for reelection against Republican Benjamin Harrison. Although Cleveland won more popular votes, Harrison was the winner with the deciding Electoral College. Cleveland left Washington to reside in New York City, where his wife gave birth to their first child, known as Baby Ruth (a candy bar was named after her). He would run for president again—and win—in 1892.

Benjamin Harrison

August 20, 1833 – March 13, 1901

Political party: Republican

Vice president: Levi P. Morton, 1889 to 1893

First lady: Married Caroline Lavinia Scott on October 20, 1853. After an extended illness she died in October 1892, near the end of his presidency. While serving as first lady she had the White House renovated and improved its appointments. His second wife was his wife's niece, the much younger widow Mary Scott Lord Dimmick (1858–1948), whom he married on April 6, 1896, much to the dismay of her three children, who refused to attend the wedding. Benjamin Harrison had three children: Russell Benjamin Harrison (1854–1936); Mary Scott Harrison (1858–1930); and Elizabeth Harrison (1897–1955)

Especially remembered for: Successful foreign policy. Robust economy and a Treasury surplus in the beginning of his administration. Being a staunch Presbyterian, who often quoted the Bible and felt that God shepherded his presidency.

Benjamin Harrison was born in North Bend, Ohio, son of John Scott and Elizabeth Ramsey Irwin Harrison. His grandfather was President William Henry Harrison (in office in 1841). He graduated from Miami University in Oxford, Ohio, in 1852, and went to Cincinnati where he studied law. Afterward he moved to Indianapolis and set up practice. With Republican leanings he was a vigorous campaigner for the party's candidates. In the Civil War he was commissioned as a second lieutenant, rising to the rank of general, more by exercising political influence than any accomplishments on the battlefield. After the war he served as colonel of the 70th Indiana Volunteer Infantry.

Harrison ran twice for the office of governor of Indiana, but was defeated each time. Opponents belittled him as "Kid Gloves" Harrison. From 1881 to 1887 he served in the United States Senate, where he took up causes he thought worthy, such as aid to Indians, Civil War veterans, and homesteaders on the frontier. He lost his 1886 bid for reelection.

With an endorsement from the Republicans' 1884 nominee, James G. Blaine, Harrison entered the 1888 presidential contest. He faced incumbent Grover Cleveland. The candidate engaged in what was called a "front porch" campaign—a seemingly casual effort in which he greeted those who cared to visit him in Indianapolis—but did little on a national scale. Short, stout, and often seen with a cigar in his mouth, Harrison was viewed as having a colorless personality.

Inauguration ceremony for Benjamin Harrison. (*Harper's Weekly,* March 16, 1889)

In the election Cleveland carried the popular vote, 5,540,309 to Harrison's 5,444,337, but in the Electoral College Harrison won 233 to 168. As had happened on occasions before, the citizens did not make the choice. Harrison's Cabinet and patronage appointments were largely determined by Republican party bosses, to whom he felt an obligation to honor their promises to supporters and favor seekers.

During his administration Harrison had a successful foreign policy capped by the meeting of the first Pan-American Congress in Washington in 1889, a prelude to what became the Pan-American Union. He worked on the expansion of the Navy, the improvement of commercial steamship lines through subsidies, and many domestic improvements. He signed the Sherman Anti-Trust Act into law, although it proved largely ineffective through corporate manipulations and evasions (years later, Theodore Roosevelt would gain fame as the "Trust Buster").

The economy, in a great expansion in the 1880s (particularly in the prairie states), turned cold by the end of his administration.

Benjamin Harrison ran for reelection, but lost to Grover Cleveland. He went back to Indianapolis, where he was often consulted on government policies. In 1896 he married widow Mary Dimmick. He died in Indianapolis in 1901.

Benjamin Harrison and his Cabinet. Seated, left to right: William H.H. Miller, attorney general; President Harrison; John Wanamaker, postmaster general; James G. Blaine, secretary of state. Standing: John W. Noble, secretary of the interior; William Windom, secretary of the Treasury; Jeremiah M. Rusk, secretary of agriculture; Redfield Proctor, secretary of war; Benjamin F. Tracy, secretary of the Navy. (*Judge,* March 9, 1889)

Grover Cleveland

March 18, 1837 – June 24, 1908

Political party: Democratic

Vice president: Adlai E. Stevenson, 1893 to 1897

First lady: Frances Folsom Cleveland (see details under 22nd presidency)

Especially remembered for: Being the only president to serve two non-consecutive terms (a State Department ruling held that as his terms were not together, he should be considered as both the 22nd and 24th president). His work to repeal the Sherman Silver Purchase Act. Maintaining financial stability while gold reserves were being drained to overseas.

In the presidential election year 1892 the American economy had the chills, a weakness that would lead to the depression of 1893. The political issue of the day was the "silver question," which pitted those who preferred gold against those who wanted the government to coin silver in unlimited quantities. Ever since the early 1870s, the price of silver metal had fallen steadily, while at the same time supplies increased due to demonetization of silver by European countries and more discoveries of silver ore in the United States. Democrats wanted Uncle Sam to bail out the market, while Republicans generally advocated gold as the prime monetary unit. Fearing that if the Democrats won, America's overseas debts would be paid in devalued silver, many financial interests withdrew gold coins from the Treasury, depleting reserves.

The groundswell of popular support was with the Democrats, as many citizens felt that support of silver would spur the sagging economy. In the presidential contest of 1892, Grover Cleveland (who had won the 1884 election but lost in 1888 to Benjamin Harrison) ran again. Harrison, seeking reelection, lost.

Cleveland entered the White House in March 1893 with the country in deep trouble. Business failures were spreading widely, and there was great distress in particular in the prairie states, where a decade of runaway inflation and prosperity had ended. He was able to maintain the integrity of the Treasury reserves, and the American financial system began to improve. In Chicago, railroad workers went on strike against a federal injunction. The president threatened to send federal troops as enforcement. Certain of his policies and actions proved unpopular with fellow Democrats, including his repeal of the Sherman Silver Purchase Act of 1890. Accordingly, in 1896 he was not nominated again for president.

President Cleveland at his desk. (*Harper's Weekly,* June 16, 1887)

In retirement, Grover Cleveland lived in Princeton, New Jersey, and was a frequent visitor to his summer home on an estate in Tamworth, New Hampshire. He died in Princeton in 1908.

William McKinley

January 29, 1843 – September 14, 1901

Political party: Republican

Vice president: Garret Hobart, 1897 to 1901; Theodore Roosevelt, 1901

First lady: Married Ida Saxton on January 25, 1871.
The couple had two children, both of whom lived only a short time: Katherine McKinley (1871–1875); and Ida McKinley (1873). After the death of her children, Ida led an emotionally distressed life, punctuated by seizures. Despite travails, the couple remained close.

Especially remembered for: Tariff reform and changes. The Spanish-American War of 1898, which many felt was initiated without real cause. First president in office to be photographed for motion pictures.

William McKinley was born in Niles, Ohio, son of William and Nancy Campbell Allison McKinley. He attended Allegheny College for a short time, then gained a position as a teacher in a country school. At the outset of the Civil War he enlisted in the Union Army, where he served for the duration, until mustered out with the rank of brevet major. Afterward he studied law and went into practice in Canton, Ohio.

From 1877 to 1891 he served as a representative to the United States Congress, where his name was attached to the tariff bill of 1890. His peers considered him to be intelligent, personable, and having the interests of citizens foremost in mind when making decisions. From 1892 to 1896 he was governor of Ohio. At the Republican convention of 1896, McKinley was nominated for president, by the action of his close friend, Cleveland magnate Marcus Alonzo Hanna, who cast him as "the advance agent of prosperity." The country was recovering from the depression or panic of 1893, but there were still many hardships.

His opponent was Democrat William Jennings Bryan, the "Silver Tongued Orator of the Platte," who had thrilled the nominating convention with his speech stating that the salvation of the country's economy would occur if the government bought unlimited amounts of silver, and that mankind should not be crucified on a "cross of gold." The election contest spawned an unprecedented number of tokens and medals, mostly satirical against Bryan. In November, McKinley carried the day with a wide margin of votes.

Portrait of William McKinley.
(*Century Magazine,* **December 1896**)

High protective tariffs aided the economic rebound. In 1898, soldiers from Spain fought revolutionaries who were seeking to achieve independence for Spain. Under circumstances never explained, the USS *Maine,* anchored in the harbor of Havana, exploded and sank. Newspaper publisher William Randolph Hearst and others blamed it on Spain, and called for immediate war, keeping up a strong and incessant call for action. Congress voted to go to war, and in slightly more than three months, the Spanish were defeated, the pivotal engagement being the triumph of Admiral George Dewey in the Battle of Manila Bay, in the Spanish-held Philippine Islands. Imperialism became the order of the day, and the United States annexed the Philippines, Guam, and Puerto Rico, while separately during the McKinley administration Hawaii was also added to the Union.

In the 1900 election, McKinley again faced off against Bryan. His opponent campaigned on the "silver question" again, but that movement had lost much popular support in face of renewed prosperity. Bryan also decried imperialism. McKinley, promising a "full dinner pail" for all workers, won.

In September 1901, while in a receiving line at the Temple of Music at the Pan-American Exposition in Buffalo, President McKinley was shot by an anarchist, Leon Czolgolz. He hovered at the brink of death, while news of his condition was sent to the world by young telegrapher Thomas L. Elder (who later became a prominent rare coin dealer). Eight days after the attack, on September 14, he died. His vice president, Theodore Roosevelt, became chief executive.

"McKinley at the Hall of Martyrs": The nation mourned when the president joined Lincoln and Garfield in 1901. He was commemorated on a gold dollar in 1916. (illustration from *Harper's Weekly*, September 14, 1901)

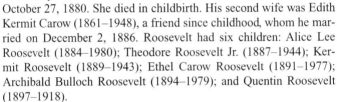

Theodore Roosevelt

October 27, 1858 – January 6, 1919

Political party: Republican

Vice president: None 1901 to 1905; Charles Fairbanks, 1905 to 1909

First lady: Married Alice Hathaway Lee on October 27, 1880. She died in childbirth. His second wife was Edith Kermit Carow (1861–1948), a friend since childhood, whom he married on December 2, 1886. Roosevelt had six children: Alice Lee Roosevelt (1884–1980); Theodore Roosevelt Jr. (1887–1944); Kermit Roosevelt (1889–1943); Ethel Carow Roosevelt (1891–1977); Archibald Bulloch Roosevelt (1894–1979); and Quentin Roosevelt (1897–1918).

Especially remembered for: One of the most interesting and admired presidencies from the viewpoint of the public. Trust busting. "Speak softly, but carry a big stick." The teddy bear, so called after his nickname, "Teddy." Accomplishment as an author, including of the multi-volume *The Winning of the West*. Originator of the terms "muckraker," "lunatic fringe," and "my hat is in the ring," among many others. One of four presidents honored on Mount Rushmore. The only president who has ever worked closely on coin designs; curiously, he has been sadly neglected as a portrait figure on coins and currency.

Theodore Roosevelt was born in New York City, son of Theodore and Martha Bulloch Roosevelt, a well-to-do family well situated in society. As a youth he suffered from ill health, but overcame it with exercise and outdoor activities, making him an advocate of, as he said, "the strenuous life." He studied intensely, developed skills as a writer and speaker, and graduated from Harvard in 1880, a Phi Beta Kappa. He then studied law at Columbia.

At age 23 Roosevelt entered politics as a Republican, and served in the New York State Assembly from 1882 to 1884. In the latter year his first wife, Alice, died in childbirth, and his mother died on the same day, leav-

Posed photograph of Theodore Roosevelt as a Rough Rider.

ing him a widower with an infant daughter, also named Alice. He went to the Dakota Territory to recover from his grief, spending two years on his ranch, driving cattle, hunting game, and experiencing the "Wild West." Among other things, he captured an outlaw.

In 1886 he married Edith Kermit Carow, who had been a friend since childhood, and during his teenage years a frequent companion on outings. She had attended his first wedding. The couple would have five children.

Portrait of Roosevelt in 1899.

Returning to the East, he served on the Civil Service Commission from 1889 to 1895 as assistant secretary of the Navy from 1895 to 1897, and as New York police commissioner. Famously, during the Spanish-American War he was lieutenant colonel of the Rough Riders, leading them on a charge against the enemy in Cuba in the Battle of San Juan Hill. After the war he was elected governor of New York State. In 1900 he was named as the running mate to President William McKinley on the Republican ticket. They won, and Roosevelt became vice president in March 1901. After McKinley's assassination the following September, the Roosevelt family moved into the White House.

During Roosevelt's presidency, which included a second term from 1905 to 1909 (defeating Democrat Alton Parker in a landslide), he took an interest in nearly every national and world situation. Attacking combines of big business that were strangling

Roosevelt's ambitions in Panama were lampooned by some as being imperialist. (*Puck*, August 24, 1904)

competition and raising prices for the public, he went on a trust-busting campaign under the previously little-used Sherman Anti-Trust Act, with great success. The Pure Food and Drug Act of 1906 ended the sale of toxic patent medicines, adulterated and mislabeled food, and other abuses. Beholden to no business or other interests, he did what he thought right for the citizens of America. He furthered the development of the Panama Canal and proclaimed the United States as the protector of Latin American countries against foreign interference or domination. As a show of strength he sent the "Great White Fleet" of battleships on a world tour, part of his often-stated philosophy, "Speak softly, but carry a big stick." In 1905 he mediated the settlement of the Russo-Japanese War at a conference in Portsmouth, New Hampshire, which earned him the Nobel Peace Prize.

Roosevelt was a lover of nature, literature, and the arts. He achieved much in the development of national forests and parks, conserving land, and public works projects. Working with America's most acclaimed sculptor, Augustus Saint-Gaudens, he set upon a program to elevate the artistry of circulating U.S. coinage to a high level, over the opposition of the chief engraver at the Mint.

On the lighter side, on a hunting trip in the South he found no game on a particular day, but on returning to camp was led to a captured bear cub tied to a tree—ready for him to shoot. He spared the little creature, to national acclaim, spawning stuffed toys known as "teddy bears," which proved to be of enduring appeal to generations of children. During Roosevelt's presidency the White House was the brilliant social center of Washington. His daughter Alice, born in 1884, was a free spirit and an independent young woman ahead of her time, who smoked cigarettes and flirted with distinguished visitors. Her father once remarked that he could either manage Alice or conduct the presidency, but could not do both.

Roosevelt was a champion of improved coinage designs. Under his guidance, the beautiful new Saint-Gaudens double eagle was created.

In 1908 Roosevelt did not seek a third term. With an entourage he soon left for a big-game hunting expedition in Africa, accompanied by a photographer from *National Geographic Magazine.* This excited the public, and tapping into the interest the Selig-Polyscope Company of Chicago created a film, *Hunting Big Game in Africa,* with nature-faked shots of the "jungle." This was a great success at the box office, preceding by a year the official film, *Roosevelt in Africa,* which was also a sensation.

In 1912 Roosevelt decided to make another run for the White House, but the Republican party endorsed his successor, William Howard Taft, for reelection. An undaunted TR ran on the Progressive ticket, stating that he was as "fit as a bull moose" for another term, giving rise to the popular name, the Bull Moose Party. On a campaign stop in Milwaukee he was shot in the chest by a lunatic, but recovered quickly. Commenting at the time, he said, "No man has had a happier life than I have led; a happier life in every way." Roosevelt's bid split the Republican votes, and Democrat Woodrow Wilson was elected.

Teddy Roosevelt stayed active in private life, writing copiously, reading in multiple languages, and adventuring. When the United States entered the Great War in 1917, the old Rough Rider volunteered to raise and lead an infantry division, but President Wilson refused the offer. TR died in 1919 at his Sagamore Hill mansion in Oyster Bay, New York.

The inimitable TR riding the Bull Moose Party—but not to victory.

William Howard Taft

September 15, 1857 – March 8, 1930

Political party: Republican

Vice president: James S. Sherman, 1909 to 1912; none for the remainder of his term

First lady: Married Helen Herron, on June 19, 1886. The couple had three children: Robert Alphonso Taft (1889–1953); Helen Herron Taft (1891–1987); and Charles Phelps Taft (1897–1983).

Especially remembered for: Continuing trust-busting and certain other of Roosevelt's policies. As his predecessor was a difficult act to follow in terms of public acclaim, and was often critical, Taft never achieved notable recognition in his own right.

William Howard Taft was born in Cincinnati, Ohio, son of Alphonso (a former United States attorney and famous judge) and Louisa Maria Torrey Taft. He graduated from Yale in 1878 and Cincinnati Law School in 1880, after which he entered law practice in his hometown. He went into politics as a Republican and gained important judiciary appointments, in which positions he acquitted himself well. He was a judge in the Ohio Superior Court from 1887 to 1890, then solicitor-general of the United States until 1892, followed by a post as judge in the United States Circuit Court to 1900. From 1901 to 1904 he was governor of the Philippine Islands, which had been annexed by the United States in 1898. Theodore Roosevelt appointed him secretary of war in 1904.

When Roosevelt decided not to run for reelection in 1908 he championed Taft as his successor in the White House, although his vice president was reluctant at first. Finally, his wife Nellie convinced him. Taft's opponent in the November contest was William Jennings Bryan, unsuccessful Democratic candidate in 1896 and 1900. Taft won handily, with the popular vote in his favor and the Electoral College votes 322 to Bryan's 162.

Tipping the scales at 325 pounds, he was the largest president in history, and required special furniture to sit upon. It was not unusual for him to fall asleep in the middle of a conversation.

Taft set about following Roosevelt's policies, but was not as inventive in the use of executive power. Anti-trust actions were pursued, but Taft did not lead in matters of conservation. In time, he disappointed many of his backers, including Roosevelt. The Republican Party became divided when the president supported the Payne-Aldrich Act, which furthered high tariffs at a time when the economy was suffering from the Panic of 1907.

In 1912 Taft ran for reelection. Roosevelt left the Republican Party and joined the new Progressive Party, and entered the contest as well. Democrats put Woodrow Wilson forward. In the election, Wilson won as the Republican vote was split between Roosevelt and Taft, with the incumbent president finishing third.

President Taft giving a speech in Winona, Minnesota, in 1909.

After leaving the White House, Taft became a law professor at Yale. In 1921, President Warren G. Harding appointed him as chief justice of the United States Supreme Court, a position he held until shortly before his death in 1930.

Woodrow Wilson

December 28, 1856 – February 3, 1924

Political party: Democratic

Vice president: Thomas R. Marshall, 1913 to 1921

First ladies: Married Ellen Louise Axson on June 24, 1885. As first lady she entertained effectively, but without pretense, and was admired by all. Interested in art, she installed a studio in the White House, complete with a skylight. Ellen died in the White House, of Bright's Disease, on August 6, 1914. The couple had three children: Margaret Woodrow Wilson (1886–1944); Jessie Woodrow Wilson (1887–1933); and Eleanor Randolph Wilson (1889–1967). His second wife was Edith Bolling Galt, a Washington widow, whom he married on December 18, 1915, amid criticism that such a brief mourning period might impair his chances for reelection. It didn't. She was a highly talented woman who added much to his presidency.

Especially remembered for: His academic knowledge. The Federal Reserve Act and the establishment of the Federal Trade Commission. His leadership during the Great War and his subsequent unsuccessful bid to have the United States join the League of Nations.

Woodrow Wilson was born in Staunton, Virginia, on December 28, 1856, son of Joseph Ruggles and Jessie Janet Woodrow Wilson. His father later served as a Presbyterian minister in Augusta, Georgia, in the Civil War, and still later as a professor in Columbia, South Carolina. Wilson graduated from the College of New Jersey (today's Princeton) and the University of Virginia Law School, then went on to earn a doctorate at Johns Hopkins University. He entered academia as a professor of political science, teaching at Bryn Mawr College, Wesleyan University, and, in 1890, Princeton, where in 1902 he became president.

In 1910 admirers in the Democratic Party suggested that Wilson run for governor of New Jersey, which he did with success, serving from 1911 to 1913. In the 1912 election he was the party's candidate for president, mounting a platform called the "New Freedom," which emphasized states' rights and those of individual citizens. The contest was a three-way split, and with the Republican votes divided between Taft and Roosevelt, Wilson took the largest share with 42% of the popular votes. In the Electoral College he won with a large majority.

In office, he backed many important and far-reaching pieces of legislation, including the Federal Reserve Act, which set up the Federal Reserve System of 12 banks and helped regulate the monetary system; the Federal Trade Commission, which dealt with anti-trust complaints and encouraged good business practices; and laws regulating child labor, among others. Meanwhile, the Great War ignited in Europe in August 1914. While America provided supplies and munitions to England and France in their war against Germany, the country did not have direct involvement.

In 1916 Wilson sought reelection against Republican contender Charles Evans Hughes, campaigning, "He kept us

Map showing the Electoral College results for the presidential election of 1912. Wilson was on the Democratic ticket, William Howard Taft on the Republican, and Theodore Roosevelt on the Progressive. Republican votes were split between Taft and Roosevelt, and Wilson carried the day. (*American Monthly Review of Reviews,* December 1912)

out of war." The contest was a close one, and would have gone to Hughes had 2,000 more Californians voted Republican. This did not happen, and Wilson took both the popular and Electoral College tallies, the latter 277 to 254.

Contrary to campaign hyperbole, President Wilson requested on April 2, 1917, that war be declared against Germany. By that time German interference with shipping, including sinking of the *Lusitania,* had become intolerable. Many American volunteers had gone to France and England to help. Still, many others had mixed emotions, with loyalties to both sides.

After the United States helped turn the tide of the war, a peace treaty was signed in November 1918. The League of Nations was proposed as way to promote harmony and, hopefully, to prevent future large-scale wars. By the time the matter came up for vote in Congress, the power balance had shifted to the Republicans, and the membership application failed.

Wilson had suffered a stroke in 1919 in a strenuous road campaign to promote the League of Nations, but recovered with partial paralysis. His wife Edith nursed him and helped with many decisions in the last two years of his presidency. He left the White House in March 1921, with no thought of seeking reelection. By that time the country was tired of Wilson and his policies. In 1924, still in failing health, he died in Washington, DC.

The silver dollar minted from 1921 to 1935 was a monument to peace, commemorating the end of the Great War. Wilson lived long enough to see the new coin go into circulation.

Warren G. Harding

November 2, 1865 – August 2, 1923

Political party: Republican

Vice president: Calvin Coolidge, 1921 to 1923

First lady: Married Florence Kling De Wolfe on July 8, 1891. The couple was childless. Warren Harding fathered one child, Elizabeth Ann Christian (born in 1919), illegitimately by Nan Britton, one of several women with whom he had affairs.

Especially remembered for: The economic recession of 1921. Cronyism in the White House. The Teapot Dome and other scandals, most of which surfaced after his death. Generally viewed as one of the poorest performing presidents.

Warren G. Harding was born in Corsica (later known as Blooming Grove), Ohio, son of George Tyron and Phoebe Elizabeth Dickerson Harding. His schooling concluded with a degree from Ohio Central College in 1882. Harding became involved in newspaper publishing, organized the town band, and was interested in several businesses in and around Marion, Ohio.

A tool of the powerful Ohio political machine, he rose rapidly in state politics, eventually serving in the Ohio Senate from 1900 to 1904 and then as lieutenant governor until 1906, but failed in a try at the governorship. At the Republican convention in 1912 he gave the nominating address for William Howard Taft. In 1914 Harding was elected to the United States Senate, where he was in office until 1921.

At the 1920 nominating convention, delegates were deadlocked, with none of the leading candidates moving forward. A group of powerful senators took charge, nominated Harding, and he was chosen. In the general election in November took a hitherto unprecedented 60% of the popular vote (16,152,200), wiping out Democratic contender James M. Cox. He went on to carry the Electoral College 404 to 127. Also in the contest was Socialist Eugene V. Debs, then serving time in federal prison, who captured about a million votes.

Once Harding was in the White House, Republican legislators found him willing to endorse about any proposal made. Changes were both positive and negative, depending upon one's viewpoint, and included eliminating wartime controls and restrictions, restoring a high protective tariff, establishing tight quotas on immigration, and setting up a federal budget system.

Certain of his appointees, most famously Secretary of the Interior Albert Fall (who accepted a bribe to lease federal oil lands at Teapot Dome, Wyoming, to private interests), engaged in illegal and corrupt practices, causing rumors of scandal to swirl through Washington. Harding, whose personal life had its own scandals, was at a loss as to what to do. In the summer of 1923, in company with his honest and helpful secretary of commerce, Herbert Hoover, he took a train trip to the West. Depressed and weary, he discussed the brewing scandals with Hoover, who advised that investigations should be made and the findings publicized, after which the matters might be laid to rest. No such opportunity occurred, and in San Francisco on August 2, the president died of a heart attack, with later rumors surfacing that he may have been poisoned. He was succeeded in the office by vice president Calvin Coolidge.

Calvin Coolidge

July 4, 1872 – January 5, 1933

Political party: Republican

Vice president: None 1923 to 1925; Charles Dawes, 1925 to 1929

First lady: Married Grace Anna Goodhue on October 4, 1905. During her stint as first lady the White House was no longer a social center for lavish parties and dinners. The couple had two children: John Coolidge (1906–2000); and Calvin Coolidge Jr. (1908–1924).

Especially remembered for: An era of prosperity, the "Roaring Twenties." A "do-nothing" president. Nickname: "Silent Cal."

Calvin Coolidge was born in Plymouth, Vermont, son of John Calvin and Victoria Josephine Moor Coolidge. His father kept a general store in the village. Calvin graduated with honors from Amherst College (Northampton, Massachusetts) in 1895, and set up a law practice in the same city. In 1899 he was elected as a city councilman, launching a political career that would see him elected to the State Legislature, as mayor of Northampton, as lieutenant governor of the state, and in 1919 and 1920 governor. In 1920 he was vice president on the winning Harding ticket.

In the wee hours of the morning on August 3, 1923, while visiting in Vermont, he received a message of Harding's death. With the light of a kerosene lamp his father, a notary public, administrated the oath of office, and Coolidge became president.

Of unquestioned character, Coolidge was faced with a rapidly unfolding scenario of scandals and other wrongdoings surfacing from the Harding administration. Alfred E. Smith, a leading Democrat prominent in New York, commented that the presidency had "reached the lowest ebb in our history," and that it was Coolidge's challenge to restore dignity and prestige to the nation's highest office.

Coolidge was readily accessible to friends, politicians of both parties, and others who sought to visit. Most of the time he let others do the talking. Famous for his quiet nature and lack of expression, he was known as "Silent Cal" and "the Great Stone Face," the last from the famous natural icon in the White Mountains of New Hampshire. Theodore Roosevelt's daughter Alice suggested that he had been "weaned on a pickle." At a dinner party a guest seated nearby told him that she had bet that she could get him to say at least three words. "You lose!" he replied.

Wisely, Coolidge let the ongoing scandal investigations take their course, without interference. In the meantime, the nation had recovered from the economic depression of 1921 and was enjoying unprecedented "Coolidge prosperity," the "Roaring Twenties," replete with speakeasies and Prohibition bathtub gin, finely

Calvin Coolidge accepts the Republican party's nomination for president, 1924.

appointed luxury automobiles, the Charleston, jazz, and other good times. Seeking reelection in 1924, Coolidge was a popular candidate and landed more than 54% of the popular vote.

In his second administration the economy went onward and upward. The Florida land boom quieted in 1925, then went silent, but was more than compensated by a heightened pitch in the value of investment securities. It was an era of expansion and continuing good times. In 1926 political pundit Walter Lippman commented that Coolidge had a talent for "effectively doing nothing." Perhaps that was ideal for his era, when America was recovering from the Great War, an economic recession, and political scandals.

After leaving the White House Calvin Coolidge led a quiet life in retirement. He died in Northampton, Massachusetts, in January 1933.

George Washington and Calvin Coolidge depicted on the 1926 Sesquicentennial of American Independence commemorative half dollar-one of several instances in which living Americans have been depicted on current coinage.

Herbert Hoover

August 10, 1874 – October 20, 1964

Political party: Republican

Vice president: Charles Curtis, 1929 to 1933

First lady: Married Lou Henry on February 10, 1899. The couple had two children: Herbert Clark Hoover (1903–1969) and Allan Henry Hoover (1907–1993).

Especially remembered for: Aiding in the recovery of Europe after the Great War. Establishing the Reconstruction Finance Corporation in an unsuccessful attempt to end the economic Depression, for which many held him responsible.

Herbert Hoover was born in West Branch, Iowa, son of Jesse Clark and Hulda Randall Minthorn Hoover. His father was a blacksmith, and the family was affiliated with the Society of Friends (Quakers). Much of his youth was spent in Oregon. He enrolled in the Leland Stanford, Jr. University (today's Stanford University) in 1891, the year it opened, graduating with a degree in mining engineering in 1895.

Hoover married Lou Henry in 1899, after which the couple went to China, where he became the most important engineer in that rapidly developing country. In pursuit of the mining business they went to Europe, Asia, Africa, and elsewhere, accompanied by their sons. By the 1910s Hoover was a multimillionaire.

In the summer of 1914 he was in London when the Great War broke out. The American consul sought his help in facilitating the return of more than 100,000 American tourists to the United States. That done, he aided in the feeding of starving citizens of Belgium, which had been occupied by German troops. When America entered the war in 1917, Hoover was named to be in charge of the Food Administration, to supply military and relief needs overseas without hardships or rationing on the home front. Conservation and careful management worked well, and his efforts brought him great praise. After the war he headed the American Relief Administration, to feed starving millions in Europe, and, amid criticism, people suffering under the Bolshevik regime in Soviet Russia. Next, he served as secretary of commerce under President Harding and was continued in the post by Harding's successor, Coolidge.

In the 1928 presidential election, after Coolidge famously said, "I do not choose to run," Hoover became the Republican candidate, riding on a wave of economic prosperity. He wiped out his Democratic opponent, Albert E. Smith, by 444 electoral votes to 87.

Building on excessive speculation and securities prices unsupported by any reasonable expectations of earnings, the stock market collapsed in October 1929, just eight months after Hoover entered the White House. The good times were over, and the remainder of his term was spent trying to solve unemployment, business failures, banking crises, and other ever-increasing problems.

Front of the camp set up on the Mall, near the Capitol building, by bonus marchers from New York City. (Signal Corps photographer Theodor Horydczak / Library of Congress)

His critics stated that he remained isolated with gala dinners at the White House while citizens were starving. Temporary settlements of shacks and tents were often called *Hoovervilles*, and a newspaper used for warmth was called a *Hoover blanket*. Without question, the president managed many things poorly, including directing the destruction of a temporary camp set up by veterans of the Great War who came to the capital to seek pension funds. "Prosperity cannot be restored by raids upon the public Treasury," he stated, in defense of his position that people should help themselves with the aid of private business, and that relief was not the government's responsibility.

In 1932 Hoover sought reelection, opposed by Franklin D. Roosevelt on the Democratic ticket. Roosevelt and many others blamed Hoover for the continuing effects of the deepening Depression. FDR won in a landslide.

Hoover was a sharp critic of the Roosevelt administration. Afterward, he was respected as an elder statesman. In 1947 President Harry S Truman named him to a commission, which he chaired, to reorganize the executive branch of government and its departments. Hoover wrote extensively and was often consulted on matters of national interest. He died in New York City in 1964, highly respected and honored.

**Portrait of Herbert C. Hoover.
(American Bank Note Company)**

Franklin Delano Roosevelt

January 30, 1882 – April 12, 1945

Political party: Democratic

Vice president: John Nance Garner, 1933 to 1941; Henry A. Wallace, 1941 to 1945; Harry S Truman, 1945

First lady: Married a cousin, Eleanor Roosevelt, on March 17, 1905. She became one of the most prominent and accomplished first ladies in American history, although the relationship with her husband was difficult at best, and in later years devoid of romance. He developed other liaisons. The couple had five children: Anna Eleanor Roosevelt (1906–1975); James Roosevelt (1907–1991); Elliott Roosevelt (1910–1990); Franklin Delano Roosevelt Jr. (1914–1988); and John Aspinwall Roosevelt (1916–1981).

Especially remembered for: Inaugural address comment: "The only thing we have to fear is fear itself." Establishment of federal agencies during the Depression, such as TVA, CCC, and SEC, called "alphabet soup." "Fireside chat" radio broadcasts to the public. Trying to pack the Supreme Court with his favorites. Lifting the country from the Depression. Quiet suffering with poliomyelitis. Brilliant conduct of World War II with domestic and foreign policies. Planning to establish the United Nations. A candidate for the most accomplished president, although not without many detractors. Only president for more than two terms. Nickname: "FDR."

Franklin D. Roosevelt was born in Hyde Park, New York, son of James and Sara Delano Roosevelt, members of a prominent family. He was a fifth cousin to Theodore Roosevelt. Franklin graduated from Harvard in 1903, then went to Columbia law school, where he flunked several courses and was so bored he dropped out. Despite this, he learned enough to pass the bar exam, and soon he was affiliated with a prominent law firm.

Like his cousin Theodore, he entered politics. Unlike Theodore, he became a Democrat. New York politicians admired his handsome appearance, intelligence, and fine manner, and persuaded him to run for the State Legislature. His bid was successful, and he served from 1911 to 1913, followed by a position as assistant secretary of the Navy, 1913 to 1920. In 1920 he was on the national ticket as vice president, but the Democrats lost to Harding.

In August 1921 a worse setback occurred. While swimming in cold water near Campobello Island, New Brunswick, where he had a summer home, he became chilled and sustained cramps. When he tried to stand, his legs would not support him. After some confusion, he was diagnosed with poliomyelitis. He was confined to a wheel-

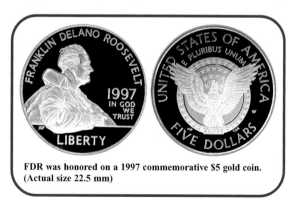

FDR was honored on a 1997 commemorative $5 gold coin. (Actual size 22.5 mm)

chair. Undaunted, he set about a regimen of exercise and recovery, including bathing at Warm Springs, a Georgia spa. At first he could pull himself along the floor with his hands, or get up with help. Then he was able to stand with braces, and walk, after a fashion, using a cane. In 1924 he made a comeback appearance at the Democratic national convention to endorse Albert E. Smith as the presidential candidate.

Although he remained crippled, Roosevelt could get about on crutches. With great energy he resumed his political ambitions. In 1928 he was elected governor of New York, and in 1932 he was the Democratic choice to oppose incumbent Hoover in the presidential election.

Winning with overwhelming support from the public, Roosevelt immediately set about vast reforms in banking, public works, and relief, aided by his Cabinet members whom he had selected while awaiting the inauguration. His first 100 days in office saw unprecedented changes and

Portrait of Franklin D. Roosevelt. (American Bank Note Company)

reforms. For the first time in several years of national economic depression, citizens had hope. In the meantime, Republicans accused him of anarchy, unconstitutional actions, and more.

The nation went off the gold standard, taxes were increased, the national budget ran up a huge deficit, and concessions were made to labor interests. Much of this angered businessmen, many of whom said that Roosevelt's "New Deal" for the people was illegal and improper, and needed to be halted. The president attempted to expand ("pack") the Supreme Court with additional justices favoring his interests, but that was ruled unconstitutional.

Year by year, opposition notwithstanding, Roosevelt's programs worked, although not without encountering hardships, such as the Dust Bowl in the Midwest in the mid-1930s. He was reelected in 1936 and again in 1940. When World War II commenced in Europe in 1939, Roosevelt worked with British leaders to supply munitions and other goods. After America entered the conflict in December 1941, Roosevelt worked with the military on strategy, cooperated with allies, and by spring 1945 had come close to victory, by then just entering his fourth term of office. On April 12 he died of a cerebral hemorrhage at Warm Springs, Georgia. He was succeeded by his new vice president, Harry S Truman.

World War II was memorialized on a series of commemorative U.S. coins in the 1990s.

Harry S Truman

May 8, 1884 – December 26, 1972

Political party: Democratic

Vice president: None 1945 to 1949; Alben Barkley, 1949 to 1953

First lady: Married Elizabeth "Bess" Virginia Wallace on June 28, 1919. The couple had one child, Mary Margaret Truman (born in 1924).

Especially remembered for: His orders to drop atomic bombs on the Japanese cities Hiroshima and Nagasaki, bringing a quick end to World War II, and possibly saving the millions of lives a land invasion might have cost. "Cold War" with the Soviet Union. Start of the Korean War. His saying, "The buck stops here," reflecting his courage to make decisions. Nickname: "Give 'Em Hell Harry"

Harry S Truman was born in Lamar, Missouri, son of John Anderson and Martha Ellen Truman, who gave him no middle name, just the initial S (without a period). His parents were well-to-do farmers. He spent his youth in Independence, Missouri, where he enjoyed playing the piano (and considered it as a career) and reading. His family suffered financial setbacks, and he was unable to go to college. He lived at home until he was in his thirties, employed at various clerking and other jobs.

At age 33 Truman joined the Army and went overseas to fight in the Great War. As captain of Battery D, 129th Field Artillery, he distinguished himself in combat and was nearly killed several times. Upon returning home he and a partner opened a haberdashery in Kansas City, Missouri, but it soon failed. Admired as a war hero, Truman attracted the attention of Mike Prendergast, a nephew of Thomas Prendergast, who controlled the regional Democratic political machine. Truman was picked as a likely candidate and successfully put up for election as judge of the Eastern District of Jackson County, a desk job, not on the judicial bench. In 1934, when three possibilities chosen by the Prendergast machine to run for the United States Senate declined, Truman was selected by default, although he was viewed as incorruptible and not subject to outside influence.

Truman went to the Senate, where he performed well, but without distinction. In 1940 he sought reelection. Thomas Prendergast was in prison for tax evasion, and the political machine was in shambles. Truman was encouraged to drop out, even by President Roosevelt. He persisted, won the election, and continued in his post. He was appalled at inefficiency in the military, as were certain other senators, who named him to head what became known as the Truman Committee, to investigate waste. When America entered World War

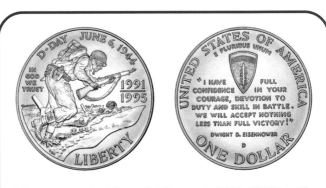

D-Day struck a serious blow against Germany in 1944, but WWII would not end until after Truman ordered the atomic bombing of Japan in 1945.

II the committee became famous for reforms that led to increased production and savings. For the 1944 election, Truman was Roosevelt's choice as running mate.

Upon Roosevelt's death on April 12, 1945, Vice President Truman became president. The war was winding down, with an invasion of Japan imminent. Truman was briefed on military strategy, of which he had been given little knowledge earlier, not even of the development of the atomic bomb. He directed that the new weapon be dropped on two Japanese cities to hasten the end of the war. In August the atomic age began.

In 1948 Truman sought reelection. By that time, Republicans were in control of Congress and most of the old Roosevelt appointees and those crucial to related programs had dispersed. Truman's hard line against the emerging strength of Communism in the Union of Soviet Socialist Republics was resisted by many, who felt that Russia would ultimately contribute to world peace. Reality was that the "Cold War" continued in progress for years. With many of his party deserting him, and with the Republicans nominating the handsome and popular Thomas E. Dewey, governor of New York, Truman seemed to be a certain loser. By dint of a strong campaign he edged out his opponent. His second term was difficult, and he vetoed 250 bills, of which 12 were overridden by Congress. He approved the Berlin Airlift in 1948 and 1949, which brought supplies to that free city, now encircled by Communist forces. A man of strong principles and determination, he led the nation through difficult and divisive times, including the "police action" in 1950 that started the controversial Korean War.

In 1953 Truman returned to Independence, where he enjoyed his retirement. For many years political observers and historians condemned him and his presidency. After his death, many reevaluated his career, and today he is remembered as a president of unusual strength.

Dwight D. Eisenhower

October 14, 1890 – March 28, 1969

Political party: Republican

Vice president: Richard M. Nixon, 1953 to 1961

First lady: Married Mary "Mamie" Geneva Doud on July 1, 1916. The couple had two children: Doud Dwight Eisenhower (1917–1921) and John Sheldon Doud Eisenhower (1923–).

Especially remembered for: The slogan "I like Ike." Truce in Korea. The Interstate Highway system. Mandated desegregation of public schools (including by sending armed forces to Little Rock, Arkansas, in 1957) and the armed forces. Outgoing personality. Enjoyment of golf. Good economic times.

Dwight D. Eisenhower was born in Denison, Texas, son of David Jacob and Ida Elizabeth Stover Eisenhower. He spent his childhood in Abilene, Kansas, which he considered to be his hometown. With an outgoing character and high school achievements in sports he was a natural candidate to go to West Point, from which he graduated in 1915.

Eisenhower's Army career began as a second lieutenant in Texas. In succeeding years he filled his assignments well, serving under generals John J. Pershing, Douglas MacArthur, and Walter Krueger. During World War II he was placed in command of the Allied forces in Europe, and planned strategies in the North Africa campaign and elsewhere. As supreme commander he took charge of the landing in France on D Day 1944. After the war, he returned home as America's greatest military hero.

The general was named president of Columbia University in New York City, then took a leave of absence in 1951 to command the North America Treaty Alliance (NATO) forces being formed in Europe to resist the spread of Communism and the military reach of the Soviet Union. The Cold War, with its threats and espionage, continued—as did the Korean War, backed by the Communists.

In 1952 both the Democrats and the Republicans sought Eisenhower as a presidential candidate, although "Ike," as he was called, had no elective political experience. He signed on the Republican ticket, campaigning with the "I Like Ike" slogan against Democrat Adlai E. Stevenson, and won handily. The Electoral College count was 442 to 89.

In 1953, a truce ended the Korean War (never officially declared as such, but called a "conflict") by setting up a demilitarized zone

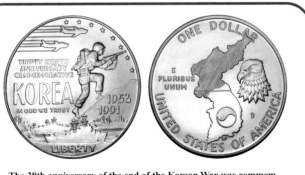

The 38th anniversary of the end of the Korean War was commemorated by a 1991 silver dollar.

with forces on each side. Joseph Stalin, longtime dictator of the Soviet Union, died the same year, creating further uncertainty in the tense relations between the United States and that country. On both sides there was much fear of an atomic attack, and during the next 20 years, public and private bomb shelters were constructed on the U.S. side of the Atlantic. In the meantime, talks were held now and again with Soviet diplomats, and on occasion tensions were eased, such as at a meeting of government leaders in Geneva in 1955.

In November 1955 Eisenhower had a heart attack. He was hospitalized for seven weeks, then discharged with a good prognosis. He won reelection against his old challenger Stevenson, this time by 457 Electoral College votes to 73. He continued to be a popular figure until he left office in January 1961. He and his wife Mamie retired to a farm they had acquired in Gettysburg, Pennsylvania. Dwight Eisenhower died in March 1969 at Walter Reed Hospital in Washington, DC, after his seventh heart attack.

Eisenhower was shown in both military and civilian profiles in this 1990 commemorative silver dollar.

John Fitzgerald Kennedy

May 29, 1917 – November 22, 1963

Political party: Democratic

Vice president: Lyndon B. Johnson, 1961 to 1963

First lady: Married Jacqueline ("Jackie") Lee Bouvier on September 12, 1953. She was one of the most popular first ladies in American history, and until her death the media eagerly followed her activities. The couple had three children: Caroline Bouvier Kennedy (1957–); John Fitzgerald Kennedy Jr. (1960–1999); and Patrick Bouvier Kennedy (1963).

Especially remembered for: His saying (borrowed from Churchill) in his inaugural address, "Ask not what your country can do for you—ask what you can do for your country." First Roman Catholic president. The Peace Corps. Failed invasion of the Bay of Pigs. The Cuban missile crisis. Family atmosphere in the White House was popular with news media and public alike—an aura called "Camelot," after the mythical kingdom, by some admirers. Womanizing, although this did not seem to affect his presidential performance. Although his administration was unfortunately brief, he became remembered as one of the all-time favorite American presidents. Nicknames: "JFK" and "Jack."

On November 22, 1963, when he was hardly past his first thousand days in office, John F. Kennedy was killed by an assassin's bullets as his motorcade wound through Dallas, Texas. Kennedy had been the youngest man elected president; he was the youngest to die.

John F. Kennedy was born in Brookline, Massachusetts, son of Joseph Patrick and Rose Elizabeth Fitzgerald Kennedy. While at Harvard he wrote a book, *While England Slept,* that attracted notice. Upon graduating in 1940 he joined the U.S. Navy. In 1943 he was in command of *PT-109,* a boat sunk by the Japanese in the Solomon Islands. With serious injuries he led survivors through the night in unknown waters to safety.

After the war he served in the House of Representatives from 1947 to 1953, followed by the United States Senate until he became president. While recuperating from an operation on his back in 1955, he wrote *Profiles in Courage,* which won a Pulitzer Prize. In 1960 he entered the election contest as the Democratic candidate, against Richard M. Nixon. The outcome was a tossup before the two engaged in nationally televised debates. Nixon appeared to be stilted and ill at ease, while Kennedy was charming and readily responsive. In November he won easily.

John F. Kennedy's brother Robert was honored by a 1998 commemorative silver dollar.

His personal warmth and the charm of his wife Jackie made him a favorite with the media and public alike. Unlike the atmosphere of many previous administrations, the White House became a family place, complete with photographs of young Caroline and John (nicknamed "John John").

Kennedy named his brother Robert to be attorney general, generating much criticism because of his lack of experience for such a post. In 1961 his administration worked with a group of armed Cuban exiles to launch the Bay of Pigs invasion, an attempt to overthrow dictator Fidel Castro. The operation failed miserably and caused great embarrassment.

Kennedy's formation of the Peace Corps was received as a brilliant move in humanitarianism and foreign relations. In 1962 the Soviet Union shipped ballistic missiles to Cuba, intending to erect launching sites aimed at the United States—the ultimate escalation of the Cold War. Kennedy, uncertain if the outcome would be a nuclear confrontation, demanded that the ships turn around. The world waited with bated breath, but the Soviet Union leaders conceded, and the weapons were returned. This "brinkmanship" was highly acclaimed.

On November 22, 1963, riding in a Lincoln convertible in a motorcade in Dallas, President Kennedy was fired upon by Lee Harvey Oswald. He died soon afterward. Lyndon B. Johnson, his vice president, took the oath of office aboard the presidential plane, *Air Force One*. Widow Jackie remained in the public eye for years afterward (including in a widely commented-upon marriage to Greek tycoon Aristotle S. Onassis) and was a favorite cover subject for popular magazines.

Lyndon B. Johnson

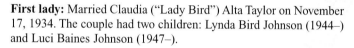

August 27, 1908 – January 22, 1973

Political party: Democratic

Vice president: Hubert H. Humphrey, 1965 to 1969

First lady: Married Claudia ("Lady Bird") Alta Taylor on November 17, 1934. The couple had two children: Lynda Bird Johnson (1944–) and Luci Baines Johnson (1947–).

Especially remembered for: A mixed legacy with pluses for the Great Society, Medicare, and other programs, and minuses for the conduct of the Vietnam War and domestic racial unrest. Nickname: "LBJ."

Lyndon Baines Johnson was born near Stonewall, Texas, not far from Johnson City (which his family had helped settle), son of Sam Ealy Johnson Jr. and Rebekah Baines Johnson. He worked hard as a teenager and earned his way through the Southwest Texas State Teachers College (now the Texas State University at San Marcos), graduating in 1930. He became a teacher at a Houston high school. As a volunteer in a regional campaign for a congressman, Johnson developed a taste for politics. From 1931 to 1937 he was a congressional secretary, after which he served his own terms in the House of Representatives from 1937 to 1949, during which he made an unsuccessful Senate bid. In World War II he served as an officer in the Navy.

Entering the Senate race in 1948, he won by a questioned and highly controversial margin of just 87 votes. For the rest of his life he would be perceived by some as a political manipulator, and with great skill. He served as a senator until 1961, when he went to Washington as vice president to John F. Kennedy, although he had been his chief rival for the Democratic nomination. After Kennedy's assassination on November 22, 1963, Johnson became president. He sought to further his predecessor's programs and also to launch a program called the Great Society—so that "man's life matches the marvels of man's labor."

Running for reelection against Republican Barry Goldwater in 1964, Johnson won with the greatest popular margin up to that time, more than 15 million votes. In office he had many accomplishments, including the Medicare amendment to the Social Security Act, and encouraging the "space race," which put the first men on the moon soon after he left office.

The administration also had its troubles, including the Vietnam War, which spawned riots among draft-age men and protests by the public. Military policy seemed to lack direction, and there was no winning strategy evident. The nation became sharply divided on this question. In unrelated problems, black Americans rioted in Los Angeles and elsewhere, in protest to the country's lack of racial justice and equal opportunities, among other concerns.

In 1968 Johnson did not seek reelection, but retired to his ranch in Johnson City, Texas. The war continued in progress, and racial tensions remained high, becoming the problems of the next administration. Lyndon Johnson died of a heart attack on his ranch in January 1973.

Richard M. Nixon

January 9, 1913 – April 22, 1994

Political party: Republican

Vice president: Spiro Agnew, 1969 to 1973; none 1973; Gerald Ford, 1973 to 1974

First lady: Married Patricia Ryan on June 21, 1940. The couple had two children: Patricia Nixon (1946–) and Julie Nixon (1948–).

Especially remembered for: Opening trade with China. Resignation of dishonest, discredited Vice President Agnew. The Watergate cover-up and scandal, indictments of more than a dozen Cabinet and key officials. Unprecedented resignation in shame from the presidency. Nickname given by detractors: "Tricky Dick."

Richard Milhous Nixon was born in Yorba Linda, California, son of Francis Anthony and Hannah Milhous Nixon. He was a gifted student at Whittier College, from which he graduated in 1934, and Duke University Law School, 1937. He went into law practice in Whittier as a partner in the firm of Bewley, Knoop & Nixon. During World War II he served in the Navy as a lieutenant commander in the Pacific and as an attorney for the United States Office of Emergency Management.

After the war Nixon campaigned for and won a seat in the House of Representatives, in a smear campaign (perhaps a signal of things to come?) against incumbent Jerry Voorhis, stating that Voorhis was influenced by Communists, among other detractions, mostly distorted or false. Nixon took his seat in the House until 1951. In 1950 he ran for the Senate, facing Helen Gahagan Douglas, in another smear campaign that unfairly branded her as a Communist sympathizer. In disgust, a California paper, the *Independent Review,* printed Nixon's picture with the caption "Tricky Dick," an appellation that stuck with him for the rest of his life.

At the Republican nominating convention, Nixon, after besmirching other contenders including California governor Earl Warren and Robert Taft, was named as running mate to Dwight Eisenhower. From 1953 to 1961 he served as vice president. Entering the 1960 presidential campaign against John F. Kennedy, Nixon was unable to get a warm recommendation from Eisenhower, who in view of the candidate's somewhat tarnished reputation told him he would have to "paddle his own canoe." In November, he came in second, after which he pouted, complained about his treatment by the press ("You won't have Nixon to kick around any more, because, gentlemen, this is my last press conference"), and in general was a sore loser.

Nixon went back into private life and landed a $200,000-per-year job with a Wall Street law firm. In 1968 he returned to politics and, based on his record as a strong campaigner, became the Republican nominee for president. In his campaign he earned votes by claiming the Vietnam war was a mistake, many soldiers had been sacrificed, and time had come for a change. "I pledge to you: We will have an honorable end to this war in Viet Nam." His opponent was Democrat Hubert H. Humphrey, who was saddled by the perceived onus of the unpopular Johnson administration, in which he had been vice president, and its conduct of the despised war. Nixon and his running mate, Spiro T. Agnew, gathered only 43.4% of the popular votes, in a three-way contest in which a renegade candidate, Alabama's virulently racist George Wallace of the "American Independent Party," took 13.5%.

Taking office in 1969, Nixon and staff, with Secretary of State Henry Kissinger playing an especially prominent role, worked hard on foreign affairs, including a gradual withdrawal from Vietnam. In 1972 he was the first sitting president in history to visit China, a country that had been isolated from America since the Communist regime took over after World War II. In the same year Nixon was reelected by a large margin in a contest in which the campaign of his opponent, Senator George McGovern of South Dakota, was characterized by disorganization and infighting in the Democratic Party.

In his second term the Vietnam War ended, a high accomplishment. Enmeshed in the taking of bribes and other scandals unrelated to the White House, Vice President Agnew was forced to resign in 1973. Nixon nominated House Minority Leader Gerald R. Ford to be Agnew's successor, and this was confirmed by Congress. Almost immediately, the Watergate scandal erupted, created when operatives of Nixon's 1972 campaign, members of the Committee to Re–Elect the President ("CREEP"), broke into the offices of the Democratic National Committee in the Watergate office complex in Washington.

During Nixon's first term, there was no end in sight to the war in Vietnam. In 1994, its veterans would be honored on a commemorative silver dollar.

When this was revealed, Nixon denied any personal knowledge. The matter escalated, and it was revealed that Nixon had secretly recorded most of the conversations he had held with his strategists and other visitors to the White House.

The matter reached the explosive state, many of his closest appointees were indicted for lying under oath, and, eventually, the playing of the secret tapes revealed that Nixon himself had tried to engineer a cover-up and had repeatedly lied to investigators. While outwardly proclaiming himself to be devoutly religious (a Quaker), Nixon's tapes revealed his language to be profane, and his ethics virtually non-existent, confirming what many observers had surmised from his earlier campaigns for the House and Senate. On August 8, 1974, with the nation watching on television, he stated he would resign the following day so that the nation could begin the "process of healing." Gerald R. Ford was sworn in as his successor.

In his retirement, Nixon was consulted on international affairs by presidents of both parties, and he gradually took on the mantle of a Republican elder statesman. Watergate remained a millstone around his neck, but he was unrepentant, and supporters praised domestic-policy successes seen in his terms (such as establishment of the Environmental Protection Agency, the Drug Enforcement Administration, and the Office of Minority Business Enterprise); his skillful foreign policy, especially in regards to China and the Soviet Union; and the influence and political longevity of many Nixon administration employees and Cabinet members. Nixon wrote his memoirs and several books on politics and foreign affairs, and traveled. On April 18, 1994, he suffered a severe stroke, later slipped into a coma, and passed away on April 22. He was buried beside his wife in Yorba Linda, California.

Gerald R. Ford

July 14, 1913 – December 26, 2006

Political party: Republican

Vice president: None at the beginning; Nelson Rockefeller, 1974 to 1977

First lady: Married Elizabeth ("Betty") Bloomer Warren on October 15, 1948. The couple had four children: Michael Gerald Ford (1950–); John Gardner Ford (1952–); Steven Meigs Ford (1956–); and Susan Elizabeth Ford (1957–).

Especially remembered for: First president to succeed a president who had resigned. Only president not elected to either the vice presidency or the presidency. Widely criticized pardon of Richard Nixon (which probably cost him his election bid in 1976). Recognized as a fair, kind, and gentle man of good principles and intent. Nickname: "Jerry."

Gerald R. Ford was born in Omaha, Nebraska, son of Leslie Lynch and Dorothy Ayer Gardner King Ford. He spent his youth in Grand Rapids, Michigan. Attending the University of Michigan, he was a star football player, and graduated in 1935. He took his advanced degree in law from Yale, graduating in 1941. Meanwhile, he helped coach the football team. During World War II he was a lieutenant commander in the Navy. After the conflict ended, he went back to Grand Rapids, where he practiced law.

Entering politics, Ford served in the House of Representatives from 1949 to 1973 and from 1965 onward was minority leader. In

1973 he was appointed as vice president to replace the disgraced Spiro T. Agnew, then in 1974 he became president when Richard M. Nixon resigned. Thus, under the 25th amendment of the United States Constitution he became the first president of the United States who had not been elected to either the presidency or vice presidency.

At his swearing-in on August 9, 1974, President Ford inherited the Watergate imbroglio, which had tarnished the entire Republican Party. Nixon remained in disgrace, as did many of his appointees and staff. There were calls for Nixon to go to trial so that all elements of the cover-up would be revealed and the full extent of the scandal known. Ford, realizing that this would be a media circus for months and a great disruption to national progress, elected to grant Nixon a full pardon.

The new president was faced with many challenges in addition to restoring the integrity of the White House. Inflation was on a runaway course, energy supplies were in crisis resulting in long lines at gasoline pumps, and the economy was sagging. Ford encouraged business to solve these problems without government mandates or intervention.

On the world scene, the governments of South Vietnam and Cambodia collapsed, creating a new set of problems, while in Israel the situation between the Israelis and Palestinians, a hot spot since the country was formed in 1948, required constant diplomacy, as did the relationship between Israel and Egypt, which threatened to break out into war. With the Soviet Union Ford negotiated limitations on the development and stockpiling of nuclear weapons.

Although Gerald Ford tried hard to do what he thought was right, domestic problems in particular were overwhelming, and the hostile Congress, under Democrat control, was constantly critical. In 1976 he ran for election, but was narrowly defeated by the Democratic candidate Jimmy Carter. The popular vote was 39,148,940 for Ford and 40,828,929 for Carter, and the Electoral College voted 297 to 241. In his inaugural address, Carter expressed the country's gratitude: "For myself and for our nation, I want to thank my predecessor for all he has done to heal our land."

Ford stayed active in retirement, especially in historical, educational, charitable, and political activities. He died on December 26, 2006, at his home in Rancho Mirage, California.

Ford's term in the White House saw the celebration of the nation's bicentennial. To mark the occasion, special designs were used on the reverses of the quarter, half dollar, and dollar.

James Earl ("Jimmy") Carter Jr.

Born October 1, 1924

Note: Jimmy Carter might not be eligible for the Presidential Dollars program by the time the program is scheduled to end in 2016.

Political party: Democratic

Vice president: Walter Mondale, 1977 to 1981

First lady: Married Rosalynn Smith on July 7, 1946. The Carters had four children: John William "Jack" Carter (1947–); James Earl "Chip" Carter III (1950–); Donnel Jeffrey "Jeff" Carter (1952–); and Amy Lynn Carter (1967–).

Especially remembered for: Being a humanitarian with the interests of everyday citizens at heart. Struggling with overwhelming energy and economic problems. Distinguished service following his presidency. Recipient of the Nobel Peace Prize in 2000.

James Earl Carter Jr.—"Jimmy," as he liked to be called—was born in Plains, Georgia, son of James Earl and Lillian Gordy Carter. His family was important in peanut farming and lived comfortably. As a youth we worked on the family farm, followed the Baptist religion closely, and enjoyed observing the political scene.

During World War II Carter attended the United States Naval Academy in Annapolis, from which he graduated in 1946. He served seven years as a naval officer, then went back to the family business in Plains. He entered state politics in 1962 and was elected as a senator, serving from 1963 to 1966. In 1970 he was elected governor of

Georgia, and remained in the post until 1975. In politics he was always an independent thinker outspoken on the subject of racial equality, government efficiency, and conservation.

Relatively unknown on the national scene, Carter announced in December 1974 that he would seek the Democratic nomination for president. For the next year and a half he campaigned tirelessly, in time gaining the support of party leaders, and on the first ballot of the convention he was chosen. His campaign against incumbent Gerald Ford was vigorous and involved three televised debates. In November 1976 Carter was the winner by a narrow margin.

At the White House, the new president inherited problems of energy consumption and economic inflation. Under his watch, interest rates spiraled wildly out of control, and much of the nation's banking system was in disarray. In the meantime the energy crisis and gasoline shortage worsened, with both president and Congress appearing helpless.

Carter was a humanitarian and sought to make the government "compassionate" and responsive to the needs of the people. He added the Department of Education to the list of Cabinet offices. Minority applicants were added to the government payroll in unprecedented numbers. Nationwide employment increased, and the federal budget was held in check. Effective discussions were held with the Soviet Union, and diplomatic relations were restored with China after a lapse of many years. He relinquished control of the Panama Canal to the country wherein it was situated—a move highly criticized in view of the importance of the international waterway.

Problems arose when the Soviets invaded Afghanistan, precipitating a war with no certain end. The shah of Iran was deposed, many Iranian businesspeople and their families fled that land, and the government was taken over by a religious ayatollah who was hostile to American interests. At the U.S. embassy in Teheran the Iranians held 52 Americans hostage. In the last year of Carter's administration, news coverage was dominated by the hostage crisis and runaway inflation. He sought reelection in 1980. The country wanted a change; Carter's challenger, Ronald Reagan, took the contest in a landslide.

In retirement Jimmy Carter went back to Georgia, where he wrote books, became a willing interviewee for the media, and distinguished himself as a humanitarian, including taking tools and working with Habitat for Humanity to construct houses. In 2000 he was awarded the Nobel Peace Prize. While he may not have distinguished himself in the White House, it is a popular saying that "Jimmy Carter is the best *ex*-president we have ever had."

During Carter's presidency the Susan B. Anthony dollar was introduced.

Ronald Wilson Reagan

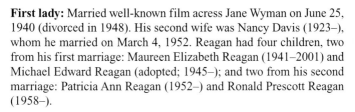

February 6, 1911 – June 5, 2004
Note: Ronald Reagan might not be eligible for the Presidential Dollars program by the time the program is scheduled to end in 2016.

Political party: Republican

Vice president: George Bush, 1981 to 1989

First lady: Married well-known film acress Jane Wyman on June 25, 1940 (divorced in 1948). His second wife was Nancy Davis (1923–), whom he married on March 4, 1952. Reagan had four children, two from his first marriage: Maureen Elizabeth Reagan (1941–2001) and Michael Edward Reagan (adopted; 1945–); and two from his second marriage: Patricia Ann Reagan (1952–) and Ronald Prescott Reagan (1958–).

Especially remembered for: His career as a movie star. His understanding of human nature, communication, and how to motivate his associates. Restoring the national economy to normal interest and inflation rates. The Iran Contra scandal engineered by subordinates. Persuading Soviet leader Mikhail Gorbachev to tear down the Berlin Wall, which happened under the next administration, leading to the dissolution of the Communist bloc and freedom for many countries; one of the greatest diplomatic accomplishments in American history. A popular and highly respected presidency.

Ronald Reagan was born in Tampico, Illinois, son of John Edward and Nelle Wilson Reagan. His father was a traveling salesman whose earnings were erratic at best. Young Reagan worked hard, attended high school in nearby Dixon, and became a popular figure, including as a local lifeguard, where over a period of time he saved he lives of several dozen people. He attended Eureka College, where he studied economics and other subjects, acted in plays, and was on the football team. He graduated in 1932.

Soon, Reagan became a radio sports announcer in Davenport, Iowa, often giving what seemed to be on-the-spot coverage, although he improvised the plays from reading a telegraphed script from Chicago or another location. In 1937 he took a screen contest and landed a contract in Hollywood, launching a career in which he played in 53 films, some of them box-office hits. Elected president of the Screen Actors Guild, he championed the rights of entertainment personalities in the era of witch-hunting for suspected Communists.

Speaking frankly, and with a compelling charm, Reagan campaigned for and won election as governor of California by a wide margin in 1966, followed by reelection in 1975. In 1980 he was the Republican nominee for president, opposing incumbent Jimmy Carter. Reagan posted an overwhelming victory. On the day of his inauguration, the government of Iran released its 52 American hostages, eliciting a roar of applause from the audience seated on the lawn beneath the podium on the back side of the White House.

On his 69th day in office Reagan was shot by the deranged John Hinckley, a would-be assassin. Interviewed in the hospital afterward, on the way to what proved to be a full recovery, Reagan lightly joked about the matter. His public ratings soared. In 1984 he ran for reelection against Democrat Walter F. Mondale, scoring an all-time high 525 Electoral College votes with only 13 going to his opponent.

Reagan worked on many fronts, including restoring the economy, easing the energy crisis, building national defense including a proposed anti-missile protection system (dubbed "Star Wars" by critics), and income-tax code reform. His effective negotiations with Soviet leader Mikhail Gorbachev led to the tearing down of the wall around Berlin, which happened early in the next administration, and the dissolution of the Communist bloc. With this came independence for Eastern European countries as well as various states within the Soviet Union. In Reagan's negative column was the "Iran Contra" scandal, a secret plan to supply arms to those opposing the new regime in that country. The matter went to Congress, with embarrassment to the administration, but no proven direct connection to Reagan himself.

In 1989 Ronald and Nancy Reagan left Washington and returned to California, where the couple had acquired a home in Bel-Air, a Los Angeles suburb. Later, the former president struggled with Alzheimer's disease, with the public kept apprised of its progress. He died peacefully in Bel-Air in June 2004.

The U.S. Mint's commemorative coin program started up again under the Reagan administration, after a hiatus of many years. The first commemorative struck since 1954 was a half dollar honoring the 250th anniversary of George Washington's birth.

**Many important commemo-
rative coins were struck
during Reagan's presidency.**

George Herbert Walker Bush

Born June 12, 1924
Note: George H.W. Bush might not be eligible for the Presidential Dollars program by the time the program is scheduled to end in 2016.

Political party: Republican

Vice president: Dan Quayle, 1989 to 1993

First lady: Married Barbara Pierce on January 6, 1945. The couple had six children: George Walker Bush (1946–, who would be elected president in 2000); Robin Bush (1949–1953); John Ellis ("Jeb") Bush (1953–); Neil Bush (1955–); Marvin Bush (1956–); and Dorothy Bush (1959–).

Especially remembered for: The demolition of the Berlin Wall and the dissolution of the Communist bloc, after which many countries became free and independent. Operation Desert Storm (the invasion of Iraq after that country occupied Kuwait).

George Bush was born in Milton, Massachusetts, son of Prescott Sheldon Bush and Dorothy Walker Bush. A young man with talent, he enrolled in Phillips Academy in Andover in the same state, where he was among the student leaders. Enlisting in the Navy, he was the youngest pilot in that service to receive his wings. During World War II Bush flew 58 combat missions, and was shot down in action by an anti-aircraft battery, to be rescued at sea by a submarine. He was awarded the Distinguished Flying Cross.

After the war Bush attended Yale University, where he was a Phi Beta Kappa scholar and captain of the baseball team. After graduating in 1948 he went to western Texas where he began a career in the oil industry. Entering politics with the election of 1966, he served in the United States House of Representatives from 1967 to 1971, followed by service as ambassador to the United Nations for two years. Two bids to become a U.S. senator were unsuccessful. In 1976 and 1977 he directed the Central Intelligence Agency. In 1980 he aspired to be Republican candidate for president, but lost. Selected by Ronald Reagan to be vice president on the ticket, he served in that office from 1981 to 1989.

In 1988 Bush led the Republican ticket. In the November election he decisively defeated Massachusetts Governor Michael Dukakis, the Democratic contender. Upon entering the White House he inherited Reagan's policies and momentum, which he handled with extensive knowledge and experience. The Cold War came to an end, and the Communist empire dissolved, one of the greatest advances on the diplomatic scene in world history.

President Bush sent troops to Panama to oust the corrupt General Manuel Noriega from power. When Saddam Hussein, president

It was during Bush's presidency that four other presidents were honored on a commemorative silver dollar: Washington, Jefferson, Teddy Roosevelt, and Lincoln, who appear on Mount Rushmore.

of Iraq, invaded and occupied Kuwait, Bush, with the endorsement of Congress, sent 425,000 American troops, aided by 118,000 from other nations, to liberate that country. This was handily accomplished in a quick operation known as Operation Desert Storm. The Iraqis retreated north back into their own country.

By the time that Bush sought reelection in 1992, the American economy was faltering, the federal budget registered a deficit that many found untenable, and racial problems continued in several cities. Although there was little controversy surrounding the president or the actions of his administration, there was enough dissatisfaction to effect a change. Democratic challenger William "Bill" Clinton took the November contest by a large margin.

The president left Washington and went into retirement, spending time in Texas and at his long-time summer home in Kennebunkport, Maine, as well as pursuing private interests, investments, and charitable work.

Another commemorative coin struck during Bush's term was the White House silver dollar of 1992. The reverse features a bust of James Hoban, the house's original architect, and the main entrance he designed.

William Jefferson Clinton

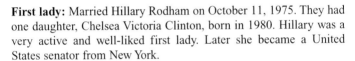

Born August 19, 1946

Note: Bill Clinton might not be eligible for the Presidential Dollars program by the time the program is scheduled to end in 2016.

Political party: Democratic

Vice president: Al Gore, 1993 to 2001

First lady: Married Hillary Rodham on October 11, 1975. They had one daughter, Chelsea Victoria Clinton, born in 1980. Hillary was a very active and well-liked first lady. Later she became a United States senator from New York.

Especially remembered for: Best academic credentials of any president. Presidency marked by excellent economic climate and relatively peaceful world conditions. Enjoyment of the office of president, with enthusiasm in most of his efforts. Headline-grabbing affair with a White House intern, which resulted in impeachment proceedings in Congress.

"**B**ill" Clinton, as he liked to be called, was born in Hope, Arkansas, son of William Jefferson Blythe III and Virginia Divine Cassidy Blythe Clinton Kelley. Three months before his birth, his father was killed in a traffic accident. When Bill was four years old his mother wed Roger Clinton of Hot Springs, Arkansas, and he later took the new family name.

A brilliant student and with a winning personality, Clinton made friends wherever he went. He played the saxophone and for a time considered becoming a professional musician. During a visit to the Rose Garden at the White House when he was in high school he met President John F. Kennedy, after which he decided to devote his life to public service. At Georgetown University he earned a Bachelor of Science in Foreign Service. In 1968 he won a Rhodes Scholarship to University College, Oxford, in England. He also studied at Yale and graduated with a law degree in 1973.

In 1974 Clinton ran for Congress as the representative from the 3rd District of Arkansas, but lost. In 1976 he was elected attorney general of the state, and in 1978 he was voted in as governor. A bid for a second term failed, but four years later he was again a winner. He remained governor from 1982 until his run for the presidency. In 1992 he was the Democratic candidate against incumbent George H.W. Bush and third-party contender Ross Perot, and was the winner by a significant margin, aided in no small part by Perot taking votes that might have otherwise gone to the Republican candidate.

For the first time in 12 years the presidency and Congress were controlled by the same party, which facilitated the passage of legislation. To most observers, this advantage was not abused, and many advances were made. In 1996 Clinton sought reelection, with Robert Dole on the Republican ticket and Ross Perot again as a third-party candidate. Clinton won in another landslide.

Clinton's administration was perhaps a modern counterpart to Monroe's "Era of Good Feelings" of the early 19th century. The economy was robust, as was employment (the highest in modern times), the crime rate dropped, advances were made in civil rights, progress in conservation and ecology took place, and a budget surplus was achieved. On his foreign trips Clinton was welcomed by crowds. On the negative side, his far-ranging program of health-care reform did not become a reality, and an unwise dalliance with a female intern in the White House led to impeachment proceedings, which came to no avail. Clinton apologized to the nation for his indiscretion, and continued to enjoy high public-approval ratings. Before leaving the White House he granted a large number of pardons, some of which were of questionable judgment.

In retirement Clinton and wife Hillary (later a New York State senator and presidential candidate herself) acquired a home in Chappaqua, New York. The ex-president wrote his memoirs, arranged profitable speaking engagements, and enjoyed the friendship of a large following.

Several presidents, and a first lady, were honored on commemorative coins struck during Clinton's administration. Among them, pictured here: the 1993 Jefferson silver dollar; the 1999 Dolley Madison silver dollar; and the 1999 Washington Death Bicentennial $5.

George W. Bush

Born July 6, 1946

Note: George W. Bush might not be eligible for the Presidential Dollars program by the time the program is scheduled to end in 2016.

Political party: Republican

Vice president: Dick Cheney, 2001 to 2008

First lady: Married Laura Welch on November 5, 1977. The couple had twin girls: Barbara Pierce Bush (1981–) and Jenna Welch Bush (1981–).

Especially remembered for: Robust economy. Warm, easygoing personality, "down home" Texas rancher style. War on terrorism precipitated by the attacks of September 11, 2001. Controversial Iraq war. Nickname: "W," sometimes spelled out as "Dubya."

George Walker Bush was born in New Haven, Connecticut, son of George Herbert Walker Bush and Barbara Pierce Bush. He spent his youth in Midland and Houston, Texas, where his father was a highly prosperous oilman. In 1968 Bush graduated from Yale with a degree in history, then joined the Texas Air National Guard, where he went into training and became a fighter pilot of the F-102. Afterward he went to Harvard, earning an MBA in 1975.

Bush returned to Texas, where he went into the oil business in Midland, with the encouragement and assistance of his father. In 1989 he was part of a group of investors who purchased the Texas Rangers baseball franchise. However, he was not particularly successful in the business world. He soon turned to politics.

In 1994 Bush ran for and was elected governor of Texas, and in 1998 he was reelected, becoming the first governor in state history to earn two consecutive terms. While serving in that post he was a popular figure.

In 2000, after nationwide primary contests, Bush secured the Republican nomination for president and in November he faced off with Democrat Al Gore. Gore took the popular vote by some 540,000 votes, with the results disputed in some districts, stirring up a great controversy. The Electoral College decided the question, with 271 for Bush and 266 for his opponent—the narrowest election in many years.

In the White House, President Bush started on firm ground, supporting a tax-relief bill that resulted in more money in the paychecks of average workers, and reform efforts in education, notably the No Child Left Behind Act of 2001. Medicare benefits were expanded to provide increased benefits and prescription drugs.

On September 11, 2001, terrorists hijacked four commercial aircraft. Two were crashed into the World Trade Center in New York City, destroying both of the twin towers and costing nearly 3,000 American lives. Another was crashed into the Pentagon, causing extensive damage. Aboard the fourth, passengers overcame the hijackers, and the plane crashed out of control into a field in Shanksville, Pennsylvania. The president declared war on terrorists, particularly those affiliated with an extremist group known as al-Qaeda. The U.S. launched Operation Enduring Freedom to destroy the al-Qaeda network harbored by Afghanistan's Taliban regime. Back home, vast changes were made in domestic security procedures in the hope of deterring future tragedies.

Believing that Iraqi leader Saddam Hussein possessed "weapons of mass destruction" and would not hesitate to use them, Bush ordered an invasion of Iraq. Hussein's military forces were neutralized, the dictator went into hiding (and was later hunted down, tried, and executed), and hopes were high that Iraq would become a free land with elected officials. At the outset all seemed to go well, and, soon, President Bush was photographed aboard an aircraft carrier with a huge "Mission Accomplished" sign in the background. In 2004 he sought reelection against senator John Kerry, and won the first majority of the popular vote since his father's election in 1988.

The Iraq war was not over, and the worst was yet to come. Continued American presence drew condemnation and wide criticism, including at the United Nations and from some of America's closest allies, accelerated when no weapons of mass destruction were found. The country became polarized, and the approval ratings of the president fell precipitately. Through the criticism President Bush remained stalwart and firm in his convictions, and supportive of his advisors.

Many great Americans have been commemorated on coins struck during the Bush presidency, including Benjamin Franklin and John Marshall, seen here on silver dollars.